THE CHURCH OF SOUTH INDIA

THE CHURCH OF SOUTH INDIA

The Lichfield Cathedral Divinity
Lectures 1950

By

A. E. J. RAWLINSON

D.D. (Oxon.); Hon. D.D. (Durham);
Hon. Fellow of Corpus Christi College, Oxford;
BISHOP OF DERBY

LONDON
HODDER AND STOUGHTON

118618

First printed 1951

MADE AND PRINTED IN GREAT BRITAIN FOR
HODDER AND STOUGHTON LTD., LONDON
BY RICHARD CLAY AND COMPANY, LTD.,
BUNGAY, SUFFOLK

PREFACE

THE three lectures here published were delivered by me in my capacity as Lichfield Divinity Lecturer for 1950 in the Chapter House of Lichfield Cathedral. Deeply sensible of the honour done to me by the Dean and Chapter of Lichfield in selecting me to be their Lecturer, I am no less deeply aware of my own temerity in having selected as my theme the contemporary history of a Church which I have not personally visited, and of which therefore I can have no knowledge at first hand. All that I can do is to express the hope that such insights as I have been able to gain through books, articles, correspondence, discussions in this country, and personal contacts with those at work in South India, may have sufficed to preserve me from major mistakes, whether of fact or of judgment. Of the importance of disseminating among churchpeople in England as accurate a knowledge as possible of the South Indian Church situation there can be no question. The Church of England has still not finally made up its mind. It has expressed its official goodwill, sanctioned a provisional measure of " limited intercommunion ", and given utterance to hopes and prayers for the future. A more definite decision is to be taken in five years' time. It is clearly of urgent importance that in the interval the actual facts should be studied and made known, and that an informed judgment should thus be made possible on the part of the rank and file of Church members.

The recent Convocation Report on South India in its concluding paragraphs stresses " the urgent need in which the Church of South India stands, and will increasingly stand, of all the help which the Church of England can provide ". It is notorious that a certain amount of financial support has been lost, as the result of decisions taken in England, by the ex-Anglican dioceses which have become merged in the Church of South India. The authors of the Convocation Report express their sense of the need for " gifts of money to meet the very grave financial situation which the Church is already facing, and will increasingly face as its work develops ". " We are convinced ", they add, " that it is the bounden duty of members of the Church of England to provide . . . such support as, in conscience, they feel able to give." It deserves to be more widely known than it is that gifts of money, provided they are specifically ear-

Preface

marked for the " South India Separate Account ",
may be sent to the Society for the Propagation of
the Gospel, 15 Tufton St., Westminster, S.W.1,
for transmission to the Church of South India, thus
helping to make good in some degree the financial
losses sustained by that Church.   It has been my
own privilege and pleasure to use in this way the
sum which would otherwise have been paid to me
by the Dean and Chapter of Lichfield for the
delivery of these lectures.

JOHN DERBY

Breadsall Mount
Derby
October 1950

printed for the 'South India Separate Account',
may be sent to the Society for the Propagation of
the Gospel, 15 Tufton St., Westminster, S.W.1,
for transmission to the Church of South India, thus
helping to make good in some degree the financial
losses sustained by that Church. It has been my
own privilege and pleasure to use in this way the
sum which would otherwise have been paid to me
by the Dean and Chapter of Lichfield for the
delivery of these lectures.

JOHN DANBY

CONTENTS

ix

CONTENTS

I

TRANQUEBAR 1919 TO LAMBETH 1930

THE beginnings of Christianity in India go back many centuries. Ancient tradition credits St. Thomas the Apostle with having carried the Gospel to India; the oldest Christian community there— the Church of the so-called " Syrian " Christians of Malabar—lays claim to St. Thomas as its founder, and its members like to be known as the " Christians of St. Thomas ". That St. Thomas in literal fact was the founder of Indian Christianity is unlikely, but the sixth-century travel book of the writer known, from his Indian travels, as Cosmas Indicopleustes bears witness to the existence of numerous Christian Churches in India at that time: and it has been thought that the Faith was in fact taken to India probably by missionaries from the Persian Empire in the course of the fourth Christian century.

It seems likely, then, that the Christians of St. Thomas have existed in South India for some sixteen hundred years. They appear to have been at one time Nestorian, though some authorities say that they were Jacobites. The coming of the Portuguese in the sixteenth century had as one of its consequences the bringing of some of them over to Rome. Sixty years later the Dutch conquests in India made possible the re-assertion of their independence of Rome, and about fifty per cent of the St. Thomas Christians became once more either Nestorian or Jacobite, the Jacobites being in the majority. In the nineteenth century a certain proportion of them came to be influenced by the teaching of missionaries belonging to the Church Missionary Society. They had, however, for centuries themselves ceased to be missionary. They were content simply to exist as a tolerated hereditary Christian minority in the midst of an overwhelmingly heathen environment. They have not come into the Church of South India. The Jacobite section of them is said to number about 600,000, and the remainder, known as the Mar Thoma Christians, is said to be in number about 200,000.

The Roman Catholic version of Christianity was brought to India in the sixteenth century, first by the Portuguese, who in 1536 established the Bishopric of Goa. In 1542 St. Francis Xavier and two other Jesuits landed in India. Roman Catholic missions in India, as elsewhere, are strong and vigorous. In South India it is said that their converts number some three and a quarter millions—a clear majority, if the figures are correct, of the Christians in the area as a whole. Lutherans in South India today number about 300,000; Baptists about 400,000.

The Church of South India, which forms the subject of these lectures, numbers about a million souls, of whom half are ex-Anglicans. The others are ex-Presbyterians, ex-Methodists, and ex-Congregationalists. It is a small Church, though it is filled with abundant vigour and life; and, small though it is, it is claimed for it that it is the largest non-Roman Church on the continent of Asia. In India the Christians, all told, are only about two per cent of the population. When we think of the tasks which confront them—the task, on the one hand, of bearing a true Christian witness in the midst of an overwhelmingly non-Christian environment; the task, on the other hand, of essaying the evangelisation of the teeming millions of India's heathen—it is intelligible that they should be more sensible of the clamant call for a united Christian front than of the things that divide them. To echo the gist of a remark quoted as having been made by the late Father Nehemiah Goreh, a Brahmin convert

to Christianity of the last generation,[1] the difference
between an Episcopalian and a Presbyterian Christian pales into insignificance by comparison with
the difference between one who worships Christ
and one who worships a cow.

The beginnings of the work of non-Roman
missionaries in India in modern times go back to
the opening years of the eighteenth century. The
pioneers were Lutheran and Baptist: Anglicanism
came relatively late on the scene. It is said that
the earliest grants given by S.P.C.K. for the support
of mission work in India were made to the Danish
Lutheran Mission in Tranquebar, and that when
the same society from 1728 onwards itself opened a
mission, known as the "English Mission", in
Madras, its agents and missionaries were Lutherans.
For a considerable period no Anglican missionaries
were obtainable. The S.P.G., which after a time
took over from S.P.C.K., continued at first to
employ Lutheran missionaries:[2] "The first in-

---

[1] *South India : The Meaning of the Scheme*, by Edwin
James Palmer, D.D., sometime Bishop of Bombay, p. 2.

[2] The Charter of S.P.G. makes no specific mention of
Anglicanism or of the Church of England, but speaks only
of an "orthodox" clergy. It is understood to have been
somewhat surprisingly held by modern ecclesiastical
lawyers that for the purposes of legal interpretation "orthodox" must be construed as the equivalent of "Anglican".
There is, however, a supplemental Charter under the terms

stance ", writes Bishop Hollis, " of the requirement of episcopal ordination for a man already possessing Lutheran Orders which appears in our records is that of Irion. He had previously worked with the C.M.S., and was recommended to the S.P.G. by Bishop Heber. That Society was prepared to accept him only if he were ready to be ordained by a bishop. This was done in 1828." [1] It is to be remembered that the first appointment of an Anglican bishop for India—that of Thomas Middleton as Bishop of Calcutta, with jurisdiction over " the whole of the British Territories in the East Indies " —dated only from 1814. The bestowal of Holy Orders according to the Anglican rite became *possible* in India after that date, but men not episcopally ordained still continued to be employed. The practical establishment and enforcement of the rule that only those who had been ordained by a bishop, and who were thus in the technical sense " in Holy Orders " as understood by the Church of England, could be authorised to minister to Anglican con-

---

of which the establishment of a " Special Fund " for the support of the Church of South India would be unquestionably legal, if at any stage the establishment of such a " Special Fund " were to become an accepted part of S.P.G. policy.

[1] *The Anglican Church and Continental Orders*, by Bishop Michael Hollis (in *Church Union : News & Views*, June 1946, published in India by V. M. Philip at the Diocesan Press, Veperey, Madras).

gregations came about only gradually in India. The more consciously correct churchmanship of our own generation may be shocked by the revelation of these irregularities, and may be reluctant to recognise all that they may be held to imply. But the Church itself, if there is blameworthiness involved, must accept the blame. In Bishop Newbigin's words, " The Protestant Churches of the eighteenth century had almost lost the conception of the mission of the Church to the whole world ". The result was that

the missionary movement—itself the result of fresh re-discovery of the Bible and a consequent new movement of the Spirit in the Church— expressed itself mainly in extra-ecclesiastical channels. As so often happens, the correction of a deformity in the Church was itself deformed by its opposition to that which it sought to correct. The New Testament knows of only one missionary society—the Church. The eighteenth century knew Churches which had totally ceased to be missionary societies, and saw the birth of missionary societies which made no claim to be Churches.[1]

[1] J. E. L. Newbigin, *The Reunion of the Church*, p. 10.

In the course of the nineteenth century missionary agencies multiplied in India. Inevitably they
worked largely in competition with one another,
and their converts came to be thought of less as
members of the Church Catholic than as adherents
of the particular missionary agency to which their
Christianity was due. We hear not only of Baptists, Lutherans, Presbyterians, Methodists, Congregationalists, and the rest, but also of " C.M.S.
Christians " and " S.P.G. Christians ". The divisions of European and American Christendom re-
produced themselves on the mission field in India,
as elsewhere, in all their bewildering variety and
confusion.

The first attempts at a larger missionary statesmanship date from the World Missionary Conference held at Edinburgh in 1910. Efforts were made
to plan and co-ordinate missionary enterprise, and
the phrase " comity of missions " came into vogue.
What was implied was a system of agreements
whereby the field was mapped out among different
and differing missions, with a view to the avoidance,
as far as possible, of overlapping, competition, and
waste. Yet it is clear that such co-ordinated
planning and mapping out of the field, in so far as
it could be carried through, would only postpone
for a generation or so the denominational issue.

There might in a man's own village be only one Church, but if he moved to a different area he was only too likely to find a quite different Christian denomination in possession of the field. As modern facilities for education, transport, and means of communication developed in India, and the populations became more mobile, the resulting difficulties came to be increasingly felt. If an Anglican convert migrated for any reason and went to live in an area in which Congregationalism was in *de facto* possession, was he to be advised to take part in the local church life and to communicate with the Congregationalists, or was he to be advised not to do so, with the risk and the probability that in his isolation and lack of church fellowship he might be lost to the Faith? It was no practical reply to this problem to point out that the whole of India had been mapped out into dioceses of the Church of India, Burma, and Ceylon, since that fact did not really mean that the whole of India was effectively covered by Anglican work. On the contrary, there were in perhaps most dioceses large areas in which the effective occupation of the territory was in non-Anglican hands.

As the nineteenth century gave place to the twentieth, and as the twentieth proceeded on its way, three things may be said to have happened.

There was developed in the first place an increasingly urgent sense of the need on practical grounds to achieve some workable form of church unity. There was developed in the second place a growing sense of the inherent absurdity of a state of affairs in which the religious and ecclesiastical life of Christians in India was in effect subjected to a kind of remote control by members of the various headquarters committees of missionary societies in Europe and in America. In the third place, as the result of a movement of international scholarship, there was developed among the theologians of all denominations a revived apprehension in varying degree of the part played by the conception of the Church in the religious outlook of the New Testament, and of the truth that there is a real sense in which the Church is itself part of the Gospel. The Church (it was realised) is the redeemed Fellowship of all such as are in Christ, and the Church ought to be one.

It is said that by the beginning of the twentieth century the number of non-Roman missions with headquarters outside India engaged in missionary work in that country was no less than one hundred and sixty.[1] In 1901 two Presbyterian Church missions in South India (one deriving from Scot-

[1] A. J. Arangaden, *Church Union in South India*, p. 4.

land, and one from America) were united into one; and this union was soon followed by another involving Churches in South India having a Congregationalist origin, which combined with the now united Presbyterians to form in 1908 what was known as the South India United Church. In 1912 the then Bishop of Madras, Dr. Whitehead, addressing the members of a national conference of missionaries held in that year in Calcutta, put in a plea for episcopacy.

I believe myself [he said] that whatever the reason for its adoption, the ultimate ground for the principle of episcopacy lay in the fact that it was imperatively needed as a safeguard to unity: and I believe also that it is as much needed for that purpose today as it was then, and that it is far more needed in India than it was in the early Church. When I ask, " If I give up this, what principle should I adopt?" I find it can only be this, that any body of Christian men and women are at liberty to make their own arrangements for their ministry. Now, I have often thought of this alternative, and it seems to me that not only does it everywhere throw open the door to division and schism, but, if we were to proclaim it in India, the necessary and inevitable result would be the creation of caste Churches. When the Indian community is freed from the restraints of foreign missionary societies, if it accepts this principle, it will necessarily and inevitably take the lines of least resistance, and then we shall see in India divisions based on caste, far more numerous and infinitely worse than anything that the Church has yet seen in the east or west. [1]

Seven years later—that is to say, in 1919—there was held at Tranquebar, in South India, a conference of South Indian ministers of various denominations in connexion with an evangelistic forward movement under the auspices of the National Missionary Council and, by arrangement with the promoters, there was summoned to meet in the same place on the two subsequent days a church union conference under the presidency of the Indian Bishop of Dornakal, Dr. V. S. Azariah. At this Conference papers were read by Wesleyan, Lutheran, South India United Church, and Anglican speakers: the upshot was an agreed statement, drawn up on the second day of the conference, which became the basis of the movement for further South Indian Church unity.

[1] Quoted by A. J. Arangaden (*op. cit.*, p. 7) from C. H. Robinson, *History of Christian Missions*, p. 503.

The statement began with the affirmation that
" union is the will of God ", and with a reference to
the " challenge of the present hour " and to the
" period of reconstruction " then beginning after
the First World War. Its authors—in number
thirty-two, of whom all save two were Indians by
race—went on to use words which have become
famous:

> We face together [they wrote] the titanic task
> of the winning of India for Christ—one fifth of
> the human race. And yet, confronted by such
> an overwhelming responsibility, we find our-
> selves rendered weak and relatively impotent by
> our unhappy divisions—divisions for which we
> were not responsible and which have been, as it
> were, imposed on us from without; divisions
> which we did not create, and which we do not
> desire to perpetuate.

Union was proposed on the basis of the Lambeth
Quadrilateral, the four fundamental principles, or
terms of agreement, being laid down as follows:

> (1) the Holy Scriptures of the Old and New
> Testaments as containing all things necessary for
> salvation:
> (2) the Apostles' Creed and the Nicene
> Creed:

(3) the two Sacraments ordained by Christ Himself—Baptism and the Lord's Supper:

(4) the Historic Episcopate, locally adapted.

The following paragraphs were added:

We understand that the acceptance of the fact of the episcopate does not involve the acceptance of any theory of the origin of episcopacy nor any doctrinal interpretation of the fact. It is further agreed that the terms of union should involve no Christian community in the necessity of disowning its past, and we find it no part of our duty to call in question the validity of each other's Orders.

Fully recognising that we do not commit our respective bodies to any action, we individually and unofficially agree upon the following plan for union. After full deliberation, let the South India United Church, if it desires union, choose from its own members certain men who shall be consecrated as bishops. In the consecration of these first bishops it is suggested that three or more bishops of the Anglican Church shall lay their hands upon the candidates, together with an equal number of ministers as representatives of the South India United Church.

As soon as the first bishops are consecrated, the

two bodies would be in intercommunion, but the further limitation of existing ministers with regard to celebrating the communion in the churches of the other body might still remain. In accordance with the principle of spiritual equality we desire to find some means to permit ministers of either body to celebrate the communion in the churches of the other body. As one possible solution, we would suggest that a special *Service of Commission* should be held. All ministers of both sides desiring authority to officiate at the communion throughout the whole Church should present themselves to receive at the hands of all the bishops of the united Churches a commission for such celebration of the communion. Ministers of either body not desiring to officiate at the communion in the other Church would be under no obligation to present themselves, as full liberty would be claimed for individuals on the extreme wing of each body to maintain their present views and practices.

While not committing our respective bodies, we, unofficially and individually, with the blessing of God, agree to work toward union on such a basis.[1]

[1] Arangaden, *op. cit.*, pp. 10–12.

It will be observed that the proposals thus adumbrated in the original Tranquebar manifesto fall short of a scheme for full unity, and are in fact much nearer to what was proposed by the Archbishop of Canterbury in his Cambridge sermon in 1946 as the possible basis of *A Step Forward in Church Relations* in England. The South India United Church (it was proposed) would "take episcopacy into its system", but would not be immediately fused with the Anglican Church in South India into a single organically united Church. The two ecclesiastical bodies would retain their separate individualities, but there would be (it was hoped) interchange of communicants between them, and a certain measure of interchange also (in the individual cases of such ministers on both sides as might be ready to accept authorisation by mutual commissioning) of ministers qualified in both Churches to be the celebrants of Holy Communion.

The sequel of Tranquebar was some twenty-eight years of negotiation. The General Assembly of the South India United Church, meeting on Michaelmas Day 1919, instructed its Executive Committee to confer with the Anglicans: the Episcopal Synod of the Church of England in India (at that time an Established Church, and bearing that curious name) appointed representatives to work on a Joint Committee of the two Churches in February 1920. The first joint meeting was held at Bangalore in March of that year, and the second in December. It was made clear that what was to be in view was *organic union*, to be achieved on the general lines of the Lambeth Quadrilateral. With regard to the Episcopate, the delegates made an agreed statement as follows:

> We believe that the principle of the Historic Episcopate in a constitutional form is that which is more likely than any other to promote and preserve the unity of the Church; therefore we accept it as a basis of union without raising other questions about episcopacy.[1]

At the same time it was made quite clear by the South India United Church that it was " not prepared to give up the privilege of intercommunion with other Evangelical Churches with which it is now in communion ", and further that " the South India United Church makes it a condition of union that its present ministers (Presbyters) shall after union be recognised as ministers (Presbyters) without re-ordination ".[2] The fulfilment of these two conditions has been in large measure the cause

[1] Arangaden, *op. cit.*, p. 16.
[2] Bell, *Documents on Christian Unity*, I, pp. 290 *sq.*

of the difficulties in the minds of those Anglicans who have been hesitant about the catholicity of the Church of South India. It is fair to recognise that they were clearly understood to be inherent in the project of South Indian Church unity from its beginning. They were not the result of any " deterioration " of the Scheme in its later stages. It is in fact difficult to see how in any circumstances reunion with Churches at present lacking the episcopate is to be achieved, even on a fully episcopal basis for the future, without conditions of this kind being involved. To this point it will be necessary to return later.

There were *at the time* no difficulties raised from the Anglican side with regard to the conditions thus laid down by the non-Anglicans. The Joint Conference, holding its third meeting in 1921 in Madras, drew up a number of detailed statements of agreement on such matters as the Government of the future united Church, the Powers of the Bishops, the use of Creeds and the implications of Declarations of Assent, Confirmation, Marriage, Intercommunion, and the Ministry of the Church. At its fourth meeting two years later it formulated a proposal for the mutual commissioning of ministers, with a view to the bringing about (if it should prove to be possible) of a unified

ministry in the united Church from its beginning
—a proposal which, however, had to be dropped a
year or two later as the result of difficulties raised
by it in the minds of members of the South India
United Church. Meanwhile, in the year 1925, the
Wesleyan Methodist Church had joined in the
negotiations, and two years later, as a result of the
Indian Church Measure of 1927, the " Church of
England in India " became free from control,
whether by the Church of England or by the State,
and under its new name of the Church of India,
Burma, and Ceylon was from henceforth indepen-
dent of both. Two years later still—in 1929—
there was issued the first published version of the
Proposed Scheme of Church Union in South India—
the version which came before the Lambeth Conference of 1930, and which was given general
approval by that body.

The first severe criticism of the Scheme after its
publication came from the side of the Congregationalists. The Rev. A. H. Legg, at that time a
missionary of the London Missionary Society in
Travancore, who (with other ex-Congregationalists) had become a member of the South India
United Church, issued, with the approval of a
number of his ex-Congregationalist colleagues,
what was described as *An Examination* of the South

Indian Church Scheme *from the Congregational Point of View, with some suggestions*. The writer, himself now a bishop, was at the time when his pamphlet was written deeply suspicious of episcopacy, and believed that in the drawing up of the Scheme there had been far too many concessions made to the Anglicans. He was apprehensive alike as to the functions and as to the powers to be entrusted to the bishops, feared lest the epithet " Historic ", descriptive of the episcopate which it was proposed to introduce, might in practice be found to carry with it the idea of the Apostolic Succession (a doctrine which for his own part he would desire to exclude); and he was clearly also in dread lest the limitation of the function of administering the sacraments to ordained men might tend to promote " sacerdotalism ". In addition, there were hesitations about the value of Creeds; and a fear lest, in the sphere of relations with other Churches, existing liberties and rights of inter-communion might at the end of thirty years, if not earlier, come to be narrowed.

An able reply came from the Anglican side in the form of an Open Letter from Bishop Western, at that time Bishop of Tinnevelly. More remarkably, a generous rejoinder appeared at the beginning of 1930 from the veteran Congregationalist scholar and divine, Dr. A. E. Garvie, who, reviewing Mr. Legg's pamphlet in *The Review of the Churches*, differed from much in its tone and temper, and expressed the opinion that not a few of the changes desired in the Scheme by Mr. Legg were unnecessary. Meanwhile there had appeared in 1929 a manifesto signed by a number of Anglo-Catholic leaders in England, with the late Bishop Gore at their head, expressing grave apprehensions of the effects upon the Anglican Communion and upon the position of Anglo-Catholics within it if the proposed Scheme in its existing form were to be carried into effect; and at about the same time there was published also a manifesto from the Anglican Evangelical Group Movement, approving the Scheme. The stage was set for the Lambeth Conference of 1930.

The functions of Lambeth Conferences are consultative, not legislative. Their utterances carry only the intrinsic weight of authority attaching inevitably to the considered judgments of men holding responsible office as bishops in different parts of the world-wide Church, and coming together for common counsel. Their decisions (unless subsequently endorsed by appropriate authority in particular Churches) are nowhere legally binding. Their Resolutions and Reports, nevertheless, go out into the world in a published volume, prefaced by an Encyclical Letter addressed not to Anglicans only but " To the Faithful in Christ Jesus "—that is to say, to all Christendom. Those outside the Anglican Church may be pardoned (and so also may some of those inside the Anglican Church) if they regard the utterances of the bishops at Lambeth, at least in so far as they are in no way officially challenged or set aside by any Anglican Province, as for the time being holding the field as official expressions of the policy and mind of the Anglican Church as a whole.

The Conference of 1930 was able to record that it was " with unanimity and with profound sense of thankfulness " that it adopted the Resolutions which it did adopt with regard to South India.[1] Some of its members appear to have laboured at first under the impression that what was proposed in South India was a new kind of Anglican Church. It came to be realised that that was not what was meant. On the contrary, what was involved was that four dioceses of the Church of India, Burma, and Ceylon would " go forth from the Anglican Communion in order to make their own distinctive contribution to the faith and order of the new united Church ".[2] The Church in which the

[1] *Encyclical* of 1930, p. 27.
[2] Report on *The Unity of the Church*, 1930, p. 124.

dioceses concerned would be embraced would be itself " a distinct province of the Universal Church ", with a " rule and character of its own ", though it was, of course, recognised that " no province of the Universal Church is free to act according to its own choice in contravention of the Faith once for all delivered to the saints or without regard to the preservation of the fellowship of the Church Universal ".[1]

The united Church would not itself be a part of the Anglican Communion; but (it was emphatically added) this fact would not " involve anything in the nature of schism ", inasmuch as the fact of the formation of the united Church would " not deprive any members of the united Church, whether Bishops, Clergy or Laity, of any privilege of communion which they have hitherto enjoyed with the Church of England and with Churches in communion with it ".[2] It was observed as " a novel feature in the South Indian Scheme that a complete agreement between the uniting Churches on certain points of doctrine and practice " was " not expected to be reached before the inauguration of the union ", the promoters of the Scheme holding that unity would be " reached gradually and more

[1] Report on *The Unity of the Church*, 1930, p. 124.
[2] *Ibid.*, p. 125.

securely by the interaction of the different elements in the united Church upon one another ". Only, therefore, when the unification resulting from that interaction had become complete would it be possible for a final judgment to be pronounced. The Conference, therefore, " without attempting . . . to pronounce such judgment now ", expressed to " our brethren in India " its " strong desire that, as soon as the negotiations are successfully completed, the venture should be made and the union inaugurated ".

> We hope [it was added] that it will lead to the emergence of a part of the body of Christ which will possess a new combination of the riches that are His. In this hope we ask the Churches of our Communion to stand by our brethren in India, while they make this experiment, with generous good-will.[1]

So, in the Encyclical issued by the Conference, it was said of the future Church of South India:

> It will have a very real intercommunion with the Churches of the Anglican Communion, though for a time that intercommunion will be limited in certain directions by their rules. Its Bishops will be received as Bishops by these

[1] *Resolutions*, 1930, p. 51.

Churches. Its episcopally ordained ministers—a continually increasing number—will be entitled under the usual rules to administer the communion in the Churches of the Anglican Communion. Its communicants will be entitled to communicate with the Churches of the Anglican Communion, except in cases forbidden by the rules of these Churches. On the other hand no right to minister in the Churches of the Anglican Communion will be acquired by those ministers who have not been episcopally ordained.[1]

In the context of an attitude thus generally approving the Scheme, the bishops considered a number of special points, and advised on them as follows:

(1) It was agreed that, provided that the episcopate, with its proper functions assigned to it, were accepted, the members of the new Church should not be required to accept any one particular interpretation of it.

(2) Approval was also given to the method of proceeding by means of a pledge to respect existing traditions, a plea being entered that, in view of the Preface to the Ordinal and the inherited rules of the

[1] *Encyclical*, 1930, p. 27.

Anglican Church, an episcopally ordained ministry for the due administration of Holy Communion would be preserved for those congregations which had in the past been bound by that rule.

(3) The intention that eventually every minister exercising a permanent ministry in the united Church would be an episcopally ordained minister was welcomed. It was asked that in the actual wording of the Scheme this intention should be affirmed unambiguously, and that " the words referring to possible exceptions after the period of thirty years, which are left to the judgment of the united Church at that time, should be so modified as to make it clear that the intention is to reach finality in the unification of the ministry of the united Church ".

(4) Assent was given to the provision that the acceptance of Confirmation should not be insisted on as a pre-requisite term of union: but its use was earnestly commended " both because of its association from the time of the Apostles with the gift of the Holy Spirit, and also because of the benefit which it has bestowed on individual members of our Church and the enrichment which it brings to the pastoral ministry of the Bishop ".

(5) The anomaly whereby the united Church, though itself in principle and increasingly in practice episcopalian, would yet be in communion with non-

episcopal Churches (described by the bishops as
" bodies not in communion with the Anglican
Communion ") and at the same time in at least
partial communion with the Anglican Communion
itself, was recognised frankly but was regarded as
constituting, in the context of " a movement
towards general and complete union ", such a
situation as might be covered by the principle of
" economy ",[1] so that there need be, from this
point of view, " no bar to the Church of India
taking such action " as it might " think right ".

(6) Consecration of bishops *per saltum* was
declared to be normally undesirable but not invalid,
and was held to be in the special circumstances
justifiable in connexion with the inauguration of the
united Church.

(7) Confirmation, normally and rightly required
in the Anglican Communion as a pre-requisite of
Ordination, had nevertheless not been always regarded as an indispensable preliminary to Ordination as priest or Consecration as bishop,[2] so that
the Conference was unable to see sufficient ground

[1] A footnote is added to the effect that " ' Economy ' is
a technical term representing administrative action to meet a
temporary situation without prejudice to any principle of
ecclesiastical order ".

[2] A reference is given to S. Thomas Aquinas, *Summa
Theologica*, Pt. III, *Supp.* Q. XXXV. A. 4.

for urging the Episcopal Synod of the Church in India to insist on it as a necessary part of the initial agreement.

(8) The participation of presbyters in the laying-on of hands at the inaugural service for the consecration of the first batch of new bishops was regarded as a legitimate piece of symbolism expressing the full concurrence of the uniting Churches and the coming together of their ministries; such participation in subsequent episcopal consecrations the bishops regarded as meaningless from the point of view of Anglicanism, and they preferred that it be not adopted and that in any case it should be made plain that such presbyters would not take part as consecrators.

(9) Some hesitation was expressed about the propriety of the granting by bishops of authorisation by licence to non-episcopally ordained ministers to act as presbyters, and the suggestion was made that such ministers, having accepted the Basis of Union and Constitution of the united Church and agreeing to work under the pastoral oversight of the bishop, might then be allowed to minister without licence: but it was agreed that the Conference's Committee on Unity would be "unwilling to condemn the action of the Church of India, Burma, and Ceylon", if with its consent

the bishops of South India did license such ministers.[1]

It will be recognised, I think, that the bishops at the Lambeth Conference of 1930 had foreseen and considered all or most of the points of difficulty in the South Indian Scheme from the point of view of the traditions and outlook of Anglicanism. A final judgment, in view of the as yet provisional character of the Scheme and the possibility of further alterations, of necessity had to be reserved; and it was explicitly stated that " the representatives of the Anglican Communion " assembled in the Conference were " not ready to express approval of every detail of the Scheme ".[2] Yet it was clear that, in general, a favourable verdict had been expressed, and that the representatives of the Church of India, Burma, and Ceylon had been given strong encouragement to proceed with the project.

[1] For the substance of the above paragraphs numbered respectively (1) to (9) see Lambeth Conference, 1930, *Report on the Unity of the Church*, pp. 127–129.

[2] *Ibid.*, p. 125.

II

LAMBETH 1930 TO MADRAS 1947

IF it had been possible to proceed at once after the Lambeth Conference of 1930, and to bring the proposed Church of South India as then planned into immediate existence, it is probable that, so far as the Anglican Communion is concerned, the *fait accompli* would have been accepted with at least relative ecclesiastical calm. In actual fact it was not found possible to proceed at that pace, nor did the chief opposition to the Scheme at that stage come from the Anglicans. It was the non-Anglicans who were uneasy and critical. Vocal opposition came chiefly from the ex-Congregationalist members of the South India United Church, many of whom were afraid lest their heritage of spiritual liberty might, under the Scheme, be imperilled. They were disturbed especially by four things—the failure of the Scheme to give expression to what was described as the principle of the absolute equality of all ministers of the negotiating Churches, the powers proposed to be vested in the bishops, the acceptance of Creeds, and the denial to laymen of the right to celebrate Holy Communion.

During the seventeen years between Lambeth 1930 and the eventual inauguration on 29 September 1947 of the united Church of South India there was much discussion and tension, in the course of which not a few changes were from time to time made in successive editions of the Scheme. Many of the alterations were trivial, but a few were of major importance, and successive versions of the Scheme were on two occasions (in 1938 and in 1943) referred to the Consultative Body of the Lambeth Conference for advice. On the first occasion the Consultative Body believed that, with one possible exception (that of the provision which made it a theoretical, though remote, possibility that, under the Constitution, the House of Bishops might be over-ruled in a matter of faith or of order), the changes introduced since 1930 were not such as to give ground for supposing that the Lambeth Conference, when it next assembled, would wish to reconsider the general approval given in 1930. On the second occasion the Consultative Body noted that, while some of the new modifications were improvements, others were not, but did not on the whole see reason to modify its former verdict.

The years 1932, 1935, and 1939 were critical. In 1932 an apparent deadlock between those who wished definitely to preclude at the end of thirty years any further admission of ministers not episcopally ordained into the Church, and those who in the interests of continued fellowship with non-episcopal Churches desired to keep the door open, was resolved only by the device of postponing final decision to the end of the thirty years' period. The Church (it was laid down) will itself then decide whether or not there should be any further exceptions allowed to the rule of episcopal ordination, and in so doing should give equal weight to *both* the apparently irreconcilable principles. In 1935 it became clear that a majority of the local Councils of the South India United Church were at that time opposed to the Scheme, and it was resolved that there must be some further years of delay. In 1939 some important changes were made in the Scheme, which by now was approaching its final form. Thus, there were changes made in the wording of the sections of the Constitution referring to the Ministry in the Church, to the Episcopate, and to the Conduct of Business in the Synod. Under the last heading the plea of the Lambeth Conference Consultative Body for a system of voting by Houses was not accepted, but the extremely complicated procedure to be adopted in the event of a disagreement between the bishops and the rest of the synod was made still more complicated, so as to make any over-riding of the bishops by the rest of the synod still more unlikely and difficult.

The most important, however, of the changes made in the Scheme was the complete redrafting and alteration of the section of the Constitution concerned with the Faith of the Church, which was radically altered at the instance primarily of the representatives of the Basel Mission, an inter-denominational society which was at work on the Malabar coast, and which represented the traditions both of the Lutheran and of the Reformed Churches on the Continent of Europe. The changes (made definitely in the interests of the safeguarding of Trinitarian orthodoxy as against pantheism) gave rise, somewhat surprisingly, to considerable difficulty in a number of Anglican minds, and were a main factor influencing the judgment of the " considerable minority " of the bishops who at Lambeth in 1948 expressed hesitations about the South Indian Church. The matter will need to be considered more fully at a later stage.

The Scheme meanwhile was in India itself during the years from 1939 to 1941 almost wrecked over

the question of Lay Celebration, which had been
referred to a sub-committee for report. Two
issues here required to be disentangled, of which
the first was that of pastoral urgency, admirably
stated by Bishop Newbigin in his book, *The Reunion
of the Church*.

The Church of South India [the Bishop writes]
is a growing Church, and in some areas it is
growing with great rapidity.   Most of those who
are coming into the Church belong to the castes
regarded in Hinduism as untouchable.   They
come from a background of extreme poverty, of
illiteracy, and of traditional subservience to the
castes above them.   The shepherding of these
multitudes is a gigantic task, and requires a
process of training and selection of teachers,
evangelists, and pastors which will take several
generations adequately to complete.   But in the
meantime the sheep must be fed and shepherded.
Over practically the whole of the vast area of
South India which the uniting Churches occupy
[Bishop Newbigin's book was written before
their actual union had taken place] the task of
shepherding the individual congregation falls
on the grant-aided teacher catechist.   He both
runs the school and also conducts daily and

weekly services, instructs the young, leads in evangelism and supervises the life of the congregation. It is, of course, at present quite unthinkable that each village should support a pastor for itself. The congregations consist for the most part of families whose total income in cash and kind is of the order of £5 per annum per family. They live in poverty of a kind which the Western European can with difficulty imagine. They give, in proportion to their means, liberally, but if their givings are to bear any sort of relation to the expenses of the Church it is impossible to have more than one pastor to a score or so of villages. The pastor, therefore, can only pay infrequent visits to each village. It is thus at all times extremely difficult to secure for the village congregations, which are the real basis of the Church, the regular celebrations of Holy Communion which are so vital for their growth in grace. Yet to solve the problem by reducing the standard of training required for the ordained ministry is a course which most Indian Christian leaders are rightly reluctant to contemplate. On the contrary, all responsible opinion is urging the need for higher standards.

In almost all parts of the Church the problem has simply been solved by leaving the village congregations with infrequent celebrations of the Sacrament. But in certain parts of the Methodist Church and of the South India United Church licence has been given by the Synod or Council concerned to unordained Christian workers—such as senior Evangelists—to administer the Sacrament in certain defined localities and for a defined period.[1]

Clearly, the problem of pastoral need thus described is a real one. The suggestion that the need should be met by teaching illiterate village congregations of raw converts from heathenism to practise what is for many persons the difficult art of making an "act of spiritual communion" probably goes beyond what would in practice be feasible. The real choice was between leaving the congregations for long periods without possibility of access to Holy Communion and adopting the expedient of lay celebration. The tradition of "Catholic" theology, which holds that although in emergency a laymen may baptise it is in no circumstances allowable for a layman to celebrate, pointed to the former alternative; the tradition of "Evangelical" theology, on the whole, to the latter. At the same time it would doubtless be held by the Catholic

[1] J. E. L. Newbigin, *The Reunion of the Church*, pp. 173 *sq.*

45

that, although a layman *ought* not to celebrate, yet
if in good faith, and in the circumstances described,
he actually did so, the Sacrament so ministered,
however technically "invalid", would yet by the
mercy of God be made spiritually efficacious to
such as in good faith received it: and conversely
most "Evangelicals" would hold that in normal
circumstances the *rôle* of the celebrant of Holy
Communion should be filled only by men ordained
to the ministry, and that the use of laymen as
celebrants could be justified only in special circumstances and on occasions of genuine need.

It was discovered, however, that among those
who in South India were taking part in the reunion
negotiations were some who held it to be a matter of
principle to maintain that a layman might celebrate,
even apart from any question of special circumstances: and this was the second and deeper issue
which the controversy was found to involve. The
exponents of this extreme view were for the most
part ex-Congregationalists who were now members
of the South India United Church. They believed
that, unless it was explicitly recognised that a duly
authorised layman might celebrate Holy Communion, the Church would be involved in a false
kind of sacerdotalism, and the "priesthood of all
believers" would be imperilled. The answer was

found in a truer exposition of the doctrine of priesthood. A passage from Dom Gregory Dix was
found helpful. " The Eucharist ", he had written,
" is emphatically a sacrifice offered by the Church
in its corporate unity, and not a sacrifice offered by
a celebrant on behalf of the Church." [1] So it
was laid down, in some sentences which were to
find their place in the actual Constitution of the
Church of South India, that

all members of the Church have equally access to
God. All, according to their measure, share in
the heavenly High Priesthood of the risen and
ascended Christ, from which alone the Church
derives its character as a royal priesthood. All
alike are called to continue upon earth the
priestly work of Christ by showing forth in life
and word the glory of the redeeming power of
God in Him. No individual and no one order
in the Church can claim exclusive possession of
this heavenly priesthood. But in the Church
there has been at all times a special ministry, to
which men have been called by God and set
apart in the Church. Those who are ordained

[1] Gregory Dix, *The Idea of the Church in the Primitive
Liturgies*, p. 127. (Quoted by Newbigin, *The Reunion of
the Church*, pp. 176 *sq.*, from a reference in a pamphlet on
*The Lay Administration of the Lord's Supper : A Methodist
Point of View*, by A. M. Ward.)

to the ministry of the Word and Sacraments can exercise their offices only in and for the Church, through the power of Christ the one High Priest.[1]

It came, in short, to be recognised that (as Bishop Newbigin has expressed it) " the demand for lay celebration as an *indispensable* evidence of adherence to the doctrine of the priesthood of all believers " really implies " the belief that the celebrant is *exclusively* the priest ", and thus rests upon " the very error which it is sought to resist ".[2] The doctrine of the corporate priesthood of the Church, in which all members of the Church have a share, is an important truth of the New Testament: but it does not mean or involve that the individual lay member of the People of God is without ordination qualified to act as though he had in fact been ordained, even though it be conceded and agreed (as it ought to be) that the difference between lay and clerical membership in the People of God is essentially one of order, and that it is on behalf of the Church, as well as in the name of Christ, that the ordained minister acts.

In the end it was laid down in the Constitution of the united Church that " It shall be a rule of order in the united Church that the celebration of Holy

[1] *Constitution of the Church of South India*, II. 7.
[2] Newbigin, *op. cit.*, p. 177.

Communion shall be entrusted only to those who have by ordination received authority thereto." A note in the 1947 edition of the Scheme adds that " After union certain exceptional arrangements will continue until permanent arrangements can be made by the united Church," and that " the Synod of the united Church will have full authority to make what provision is needed for the administration of the Sacrament in all its congregations ".[1] In January 1950 the Committee on Faith and Order of the Church of South India found itself able to give an explicit assurance that " All the lay persons who formerly held licences to celebrate the Holy Communion have now been given further training and ordained as Presbyters, with the exception of one senior man ", and that the " rule of order " according to which those only may celebrate Holy Communion who " have by ordination received authority thereto " is an authoritative rule of the South Indian Church.[2]

In 1941 the Joint Committee in India reviewed progress up to date, agreed upon what was intended

[1] *Proposed Scheme of Church Union in South India* (seventh edition, reprinted with additional matter, 1947), p. 9.
[2] *The Church of South India : Being the United Report of the Joint Committee of the Convocations of Canterbury and York*, 1950, p. 47.

to be the final form of the Scheme, and issued an appeal for the reaching of a definite decision by the spring of 1944. A kite flown in 1943 in favour of the substitution of a scheme for a " Federal Union " of Churches for the projected united Church came to nothing; and the same fate befell a proposal, promoted in 1944 by the General Council of the Church of India, Burma, and Ceylon, for the initial unification of the ministries of the uniting Churches by the method of mutual supplemental ordination. The rejection of this latter scheme was to many in the Church of India, Burma, and Ceylon grievously disappointing, since it had been put forward with high hopes. The Council had before it a letter from Bishops Palmer and Western (both formerly bishops of dioceses in India), who as members of the Archbishop's Overseas Advisory Committee in England had been considering suggestions for unified ministries put forward in different parts of the world, and who (adopting some words from an American document) explained the expression " supplemental ordination " as being—

intended to imply that he who receives it is recognised to have been truly ordained to the ministry of Christ's Church, and that by the supplemental rite he receives such further grace of orders, and such authority for the wider exercise of his ministry as, according to God's will, may be conveyed through the action of the Church in and by which the rite is performed.

The actual formula proposed by the two bishops for use at a service of supplemental ordination was as follows:

Receive the Holy Ghost for the work of a presbyter in the Church of God, both for the continuance of that work which thou hast done hitherto, and for the performance of that work which is now committed unto thee by the laying on of our hands. Take thou authority to preach and teach the Word, to fulfil the ministry of reconciliation and to minister Christ's Sacraments in the congregations whereunto thou shalt be further called or lawfully appointed; and see that thou do all these things in brotherly partnership with God's fellow-workers whom in this union of Churches He has made thine.

The Council of the Church of India, Burma, and Ceylon, in accepting and putting forward the proposal, expressed solemnly its conviction that so long as Christians remained out of communion with one another they were all defective in spiritual power, and that this was true in a special way of the ordained ministry. In moving words it was acknowledged that in the past those in whose name the statement was put forward had " failed in manifold ways to forward the work of reconciliation ".

> For these sins of the past [it was added] we earnestly repent and desire to atone: and we desire to express that penitence not only in words but also in action. We believe that when separated Communions come together again, their ministries should be united by a solemn act of humility and re-dedication, in which through the mutual laying on of hands with prayer they seek from God the enrichment of all those ministries.

The General Assembly of the South India United Church in reply expressed itself as being deeply moved by the document, and as being also ready to express penitence for the sins of pride, self-sufficiency, and contentment with a disunited Church. Its members, however, did not feel able to commend to the Church the method of supplemental ordination proposed. They hoped that the Joint Committee might be able instead to work out a form of inauguration expressive of humility and re-dedication, but without including the laying on of hands.

The Joint Committee itself, meeting in November 1944 in Madras, was obliged, after full discussion, to record that it had " not been able to reach a common mind on this subject ", and accordingly was " not able at this stage of the negotiations to recommend the proposal to the Churches ".[1]

Meanwhile, as early as February 1943, the Metropolitan of India, in response to a request made to him by the Bishops of Nagpur and Colombo, addressed to his fellow-Metropolitans of the other Provinces of the Anglican Communion throughout the world a formal letter of enquiry, whether, in the event of the inauguration of a united Church of South India in accordance with the proposed Scheme of Church Union as presented in the seventh edition of that Scheme, their respective Provinces would break off communion with the Church of India, Burma, and Ceylon and/or refuse to be in communion with the Church of South India. In the Province of Canterbury important statements were in consequence made by Archbishop Temple in a presidential Address delivered in full synod in the Convocation of Canterbury on 25 May 1943, and in a carefully-weighed speech in the Upper House of the Convocation on 21 January

[1] See for the subject-matter of the above paragraphs, Arangaden, *op. cit*, pp. 160 *sqq*. and p. 172.

1944. Both Houses of the Convocation were consulted, and the advice of both was taken into account, before the final text of the Archbishop's formal reply to the Metropolitan of India was settled. A formal answer, with a less formal covering letter, was sent to India at the end of January 1944.[1]

In the formal reply of the Archbishop to the Metropolitan of India it was made clear that the answer to his first question—Would the Province of Canterbury break communion with the Church of India, Burma, and Ceylon on the ground of its action in allowing the Scheme to go forward?—was an emphatic negative. The answer to the second question—Would the Province of Canterbury refuse to be in communion with the Church of South India?—was more complex. In effect, it was intimated that the policy foreshadowed at Lambeth in 1930 would be followed, subject to the existing rules of the Province, and taking account of the necessity of compliance with the provisions (where they applied) of the Colonial Clergy Act. In his statement made in the Upper House of the Convocation on 21 January 1944, the Archbishop remarked that what was proposed

[1] The text of both is printed in full in the first number of the *Chronicle of Convocation* for 1944.

was " a restricted intercommunion "; adding, a few sentences later—

For myself, while I desire with all my soul to maintain intact the faith and tradition of the Anglican Communion, I also hold that in the distressful circumstances of the modern world there is need of something intermediate between either organic union or full communion, such as the Churches of the Anglican Communion enjoy with one another, and total lack of any communion *in sacris*.

A year later the present Archbishop of Canterbury, in a statement addressed to Convocation in May 1945, said that in his view there would be " a very real and close friendship between the proposed Church and the Church of England—how could it be otherwise when " the new Church would be " engaged on such high venture of faith ", and would contain " so high a proportion of Anglicans "? —but that, in the proper and technical sense of the word, the two Churches would " not, as Churches, be in communion with one another ", notwithstanding the fact that " by administrative action ministers and members of the proposed Church " might " be accepted by us after scrutiny according to their individual status and our own rules ".

In England during these critical years there was much controversy on the South Indian Church Scheme. There were quarters in which serious anxiety was rightly or wrongly felt on theological grounds; but there were also circles in which prejudice was being aroused, and statements were being made which were clearly not based upon knowledge. It was freely rumoured, for example, that a Congregationalist unbaptised minister who said he had no intention of being baptised would be one of the new bishops! The apparent origin of so surprising a suggestion was the fact that a leading Congregationalist who had been at work in South India while the negotiations were going on had spoken and written against the necessity of baptism. It had never been suggested that he should be made a bishop; nor is it easy to see how a man holding his views could have honourably become even a member of a Church the Constitution of which definitely prescribed baptism with water in the name of the Father and of the Son and of the Holy Ghost as a condition of membership.[1] This missionary is no longer in South India. Despite his opinions, it was not true that he had not himself been baptised. There are in the Church of South

[1] *Constitution of the Church of South India*, II. 4 and III. 1.

India no unbaptised persons who are regarded as members, and no unbaptised communicants. In South India, as in other parts of the mission field, the distinctions between heathen enquirers, unbaptised catechumens, baptised Christians, and faithful communicants are more familiar and more clearly defined than they are (for example) in England.

Apart from this question of baptism, it was being widely asserted in England that the Church of South India, if it came into existence, would be " schismatic ", and that the Church of India, Burma, and Ceylon, if it consented to four of its dioceses going out in order to join it, would be " condoning an act of schism ". The Lambeth Conference of 1930 had not taken this view. On the contrary, the bishops assembled at Lambeth in 1930 had written in the Encyclical Letter which they sent out after the Conference:

> We rejoice that one part of the Anglican Communion should be found ready to make this venture for a corporate union with certain non-episcopal Churches. We feel that in a sense our brethren in South India are making this experiment on behalf of the whole body of the Anglican Churches. They are our pioneers in this direc-

tion of the movement for unity. The whole Communion will surely stand by them with earnest prayer and generous loyalty.[1]

In the *Report of the Committee on the Unity of the Church* of the same year the words occur:

The united Church in South India will not be a part of the Anglican Communion. *This does not, however, involve anything in the nature of schism*, for even though the united Church will not be an integral part of the Anglican Communion, the fact of the formation of the united Church will not deprive any members of the united Church, whether Bishops, Clergy, or Laity, of any privilege of communion which they have hitherto enjoyed with the Church of England and with the Churches in communion with it.[2]

The words " schism " and " schismatic " can be variously employed. To what extent is the Church of England itself a schismatic Church? There exists certainly a division or " schism " between the Church of England and the Church of Rome, and indeed between the Church of England and most parts of Christendom. It is sometimes forgotten

[1] *Lambeth Conference Encyclical*, 1930, p. 26.
[2] *Lambeth, 1930 : Report on the Unity of the Church*, p. 125.

that, apart from the small group of minority Churches known as the Old Catholic Communion on the continent of Europe, there is at the present time no non-Anglican portion of Christendom with which the Anglican Churches are, in the full and technical sense of the words, in communion. Are the Anglican Churches, therefore, schismatic? In one sense, yes: for they are in fact deeply involved in the " unhappy divisions " of Christendom. It is best, however, only to use epithets such as " schismatic " in contexts in which there is a justified imputation of guilt. In that sense the four Anglican dioceses which, with the consent and encouragement of the Church to which they belonged and of the bishops at Lambeth, went into the Church of South India were not acting schismatically. " The intention ", in Bishop Palmer's words, " of the four dioceses " was " not to rend the Church of God, but to begin the mending of some of the rents that " were " already in it ".[1]

In 1946 the Archbishop of Canterbury, in view of the theological anxieties which were being freely expressed, appointed a Committee of Theologians (of which I was myself asked to be Chairman) to consider and to report upon the proposed Basis of

[1] *South India : The Meaning of the Scheme*, by Edwin James Palmer, D.D., sometime Bishop of Bombay, p. 25.

Union and Constitution of the future Church of South India. Without questioning the general character of the Scheme, as approved by the Anglican episcopate at the Lambeth Conference of 1930, under which the proposed Church of South India would be outside the Anglican Communion during an interim period of " growing together "; and having in mind the hope entertained by the Lambeth Conference that at the end of the interim period the proposed Church might be received into full communion with the Anglican Church, we were to report: (*a*) what amendments (if any) we considered to be necessary on theological and doctrinal grounds if the hope entertained by the Lambeth Conference was to be fulfilled; (*b*) what amendments (if any) we considered to be desirable though not necessary on theological and doctrinal grounds; and (*c*) what amendments (if any) we considered to be important enough in the interests of clarity and good expression to be put forward for consideration.

It was added that if the proposed Church came into existence every Province of the Anglican Communion, including the Church of India, Burma, and Ceylon, would have to define its relation to the proposed Church, and that this would largely depend on the Ordinal adopted by the proposed

Church and other factors not yet known. The Church of India, Burma, and Ceylon would, however, alone bear the responsibility of allowing or forbidding four of its dioceses to join the proposed Church: and yet if, in allowing them to do so, it could properly claim to be acting in conformity with advice of the Anglican episcopate given at Lambeth in 1930, its responsibility would be shared with the whole Anglican Communion. The Committee was accordingly given liberty to consider whether in its opinion the Church of India, Burma, and Ceylon was still justified in making that claim or not in view of all that had happened since 1930, including the conclusions of the Consultative Body of the Lambeth Conference.

The Committee consisted of seven members representative of various shades of theological opinion in the Church. It was, as the Archbishop has since observed, " if anything, overweighted on the critical side ".[1] It went through the Scheme carefully, point by point; and it can be claimed, I think, that it gave serious consideration to every considerable criticism which had been brought to bear upon it or urged against it from the Anglican

[1] *The South India Church : An Open Letter from the Archbishop of Canterbury to Bishop Stephen Neill* (Press and Publications Board, 1947), p. 10.

side. Its Report, published in 1946 by the Press and Publications Board (as it then was) of the Church Assembly, has been widely circulated, and is, I believe, still available.[1]   I need not here reproduce it in detail. In its concluding section, the Report specified six points in respect of some or all of which a clear majority of its members were disposed to regard the amendment of the Constitution of the proposed new Church as being likely to be essential, if in the end there was to be full intercommunion with the Anglican Churches.

The six points were as follows:

(1) The statement of the Faith of the Church should be so redrafted as to place the adherence of the Church of South India to the historic faith of the Church Catholic beyond question.

(2) The statement on the Sacraments in the Church (*Constitution* II. 6) should be freed from misleading ambiguities.

(3) The use of the rite of Confirmation should, as soon as may be practicable, be made the general rule of the Church.

(4) There should be a modification of the rules for synodical procedure, clarifying and

[1] *The South India Church Scheme* (Press and Publications Board, 1946).

properly safeguarding the position of the bishops.

(5) There should be a reconsideration of the ultimate relation of the Church of South India to other Churches not episcopally ordered.

(6) There should be a satisfactory clarification of the circumstances, if any, in which non-episcopally ordained ministers may continue to exercise ministry in the Church of South India at the conclusion of the interim period.

It was added that there would further be needed satisfactory provisions in respect of the forms to be used at consecrations and ordinations, and of the marriage law of the Church.

The quotation of this part of the Committee's Report by the Lambeth Conference's Committee on the Unity of the Church in 1948,[1] and the fact that in one of its Resolutions the Conference as a whole called " special attention to the six points specified in the Report of its Committee on Unity ",[2] have in some quarters tended to convey the impression that the six points stand all on the same level of importance, and that they constitute, as it were, a sort of ultimatum addressed with official unanimity by the Anglican Churches to the Church

[1] *Lambeth Conference Report, 1948,* Part II, p. 44.
[2] *Lambeth Conference, 1948, Resolutions,* No. 53.

of South India, as the condition of any future realisation of full communion. Actually, the six points are of very varying degrees of importance. The Report of what has come to be known as the Derby Committee spoke of a " clear majority " of the Committee (which consisted of seven members in all) as being " disposed, with varying degrees of emphasis ", to regard as being " likely to be essential " the amendment of the Constitution in " some or all of " the ways specified; and in a later paragraph remarked that " the members of the Committee as a whole " had " not found it easy to distinguish between those amendments which they " regarded as being " in the strict sense essential " and those which they regarded as being " highly desirable "; and that " some of their numbers would go further than others ". In actual fact the Committee put into the list whatever points were regarded as being of serious importance by any one of its members, whether or not he had the support of his colleagues; so that the inclusion of a particular point in the list does not by any means imply that the modification desired in the Constitution of the Church of South India would be regarded as being indispensable by the majority of Anglicans, or by the Anglican Church as a whole; it means only that there are Anglicans who would desire it, and that by a minority (large or small) it might even be regarded as a *sine qua non.*

The Report of the Committee ended with the recognition that it was not contemplated that the proposed Church of South India should, at any stage of its future, become an actual part of the Anglican Communion. The ideal in view was rather a relation analogous to that between the Church of England and the Old Catholics.

The two Churches, without being necessarily in agreement in all points of doctrine or practice, would yet (it is hoped) in the end be able to recognise one another as each holding sufficiently the essentials of Catholic faith and order, and on that basis would be free to establish full intercommunion.

With this hope in view, a majority of the Committee thinks that the Scheme should go forward. The Committee as a whole, if the Scheme comes into operation, would desire to wish God-speed to the Church of South India, and to follow its fortunes with warm sympathy as well as with prayer.[1]

[1] *The South India Church Scheme* (Derby Report), p. 46.

The Report, duly presented to the Archbishop, was published at once, and copies were flown out to India, where the decisive vote on the Scheme was about to be taken. Already in the previous year (1945) the General Council of the Church of India, Burma, and Ceylon had, by a three-fourths majority, voted in favour of adopting the Scheme, but there had been a last-moment hitch. Included in the Scheme was a paragraph concerned with what was known as the " Pledge ". This was an undertaking on the part of the future united Church not to override consciences, and in no circumstances to impose on any congregation either forms of worship or ritual or a ministry to which its members conscientiously objected. Anglicans in India, influenced by what had been said by the Lambeth Conference of 1930 about preserving for congregations which in the past had been bound by such a rule " an episcopally ordained ministry . . . for the due administration of Holy Communion ",[1] had understood this pledge to imply that in no circumstances would a minister who had not been episcopally ordained be allowed to celebrate for an ex-Anglican congregation, even if the congregation did not object. But, after the General Council had voted on the Scheme as it stood, it became

[1] *Lambeth Conference Report, 1930*, p. 127.

known that a few months previously (in November 1944) the Joint Negotiating Committee had agreed to print in the forthcoming final edition of the Scheme an interpretative note implying a less rigid understanding of the Pledge.

> The Committee [they had written] does not understand the pledge to imply that the fact that a minister of the united Church has previously been a minister of either an episcopal or a non-episcopal Church will in itself debar him from appointment to or working in any congregation of the united Church where that congregation desires it.

The effect of the decision (when it became known) to insert a note on these lines, which had not been included in the Scheme as approved in 1945 by the Church of India, Burma, and Ceylon, was to cause the House of Bishops of that Church to make a pronouncement declaring that its members seemed " bound to adhere to the interpretation of the pledge contained on page 127 of the Report of the Lambeth Conference of 1930 ". The House was

> not concerned [they said] to assert that a minister of the United Church of South India is debarred from being placed in charge of an ex-Anglican

congregation by the sole fact that he has not received episcopal ordination. It is concerned to assert that, except in cases of extreme pastoral urgency, an ex-Anglican congregation is, under the Pledge, prevented by long-established tradition from being placed in the charge of a non-episcopally ordained minister.

The bishops at the same time drew attention to certain criticisms of the Scheme which had been made by " Bishop Palmer and others ". In effect, they wished for a further period of revision and reconsideration of the Scheme.[1]

Feeling for a time ran high in Anglican circles in India. A layman's manifesto was published, protesting against the bishops' action in meeting separately to pass resolutions of such importance without reference to or consultation with the other two Houses of the General Council of the Church. Their action, it was suggested, might well have the effect of deepening the suspicions of those who were suspicious of episcopacy, and of giving a wrong impression of the position of the bishops in the Constitution of the Church. There was added a strong appeal not to falter in carrying out the decision, already taken, to carry through the pro-

[1] Arangaden, *op. cit.*, pp. 180 *sq.*

posed union.[1]   The Joint Committee, meanwhile, published a further statement, in which it was said that:

It is understood that during the period of unification congregations will ordinarily continue to be served by the ministries to which they are accustomed, except where pastoral needs obviously demand other arrangements.   The duly constituted authority within the united Church shall be the sole judge of the urgency of such pastoral needs.

When in January 1947 the General Council of the Church of India, Burma, and Ceylon met once more, the note interpreting the Pledge which had been put forward by the Joint Negotiating Committee in 1946 was accepted as being " wholly in accordance with the Basis of Union which was adopted by the General Council in 1945 ".   The motion for the acceptance of this intepretation was carried by only one vote in the House of Bishops, but by a substantial majority (30 votes to 22) in the House of Clergy, and by a still more substantial majority (33 to 7) in the House of Laity.   Two bishops, believed to have been ready to vote on the majority side, were away.   The actual voting in the

[1] Arangaden, *op. cit.*, pp. 182 *sq.*

House of Bishops was seven to six. Since the South India Provincial Synod of the Methodist Church had accepted the revised Scheme in January 1943, and the General Assembly of the South India United Church had done so in September 1946, all was now in readiness. On 27 September 1947 the Church of South India was inaugurated in Madras Cathedral. In the following year at the Lambeth Conference the members of the Committee on the Unity of the Church were able to write as follows:

The Church of South India exists. It was inaugurated in September, 1947, amid great joy —joy in the Lord. It unites a million people. They are mainly Indian, speaking the four languages of Southern India, for the most part simple and uneducated. They have what they wanted—one Church . . .

For the measure of unity already achieved in this unique event we rejoice and give thanks to God, and pledge ourselves to pray Him to guide the development of the Church of South India into a more and more perfect expression of His will for the Church.

The inauguration of the Church of South India was the end of much that grieved the divine Head of the Body and distressed His members.　But it is also the beginning of much else . . . We set our hearts on Jesus Christ, and pray that all the members of the Church of South India will do the same. . . . They have united in order the better to convert India to Christ. Let us not fear that they will desert Him, for He will never desert them.[1]

[1] *Lambeth Conference, 1948:* Report of Committee on *The Unity of the Church*, pp. 41 *sq.*

members. . . . But it is also the beginning of much else. . . . We set our hearts on Jesus Christ, and pray that the members of the Church of South India will do the same. . . . They have united in order the better to convert India to Christ. Let us not fear that they will desert Him, for He will never desert them.

Lambeth Conference, 1930, Report of Committee on The Unity of the Church, pp. 113-114.

III

LAMBETH 1948 AND AFTER

THE Lambeth Conference of 1948 was con-
fronted no longer by a debatable project for
church unity in South India, but by a Church of
South India in being. Its problem was to advise
on the precise form of relation to that Church
which the Anglican Churches throughout the
world might be most wisely recommended to
adopt. The Conference had before it both the
Report of the so-called Derby Committee and the
Report issued eighteen years previously by the
Lambeth Conference of 1930. The sixty-six
members of its Committee on the Unity of the
Church had the advantage of spending a long
morning in consultation with two of the South
Indian Bishops—Bishop Jacob of Central Travancore and Bishop Newbigin of Madura—who,
though, of course, not members of the Conference,
were in England at the time, and who were present
at the meeting of the Committee by invitation.
The two bishops made a considerable impression,

and their explanations had the effect, in the minds of many of those who heard them, of clearing up a number of points which had been causing perplexity. In particular, the members of the Committee found themselves reassured of the essential orthodoxy of the South Indian Church, which, in view of the altered form of the section of the Constitution referring to the Faith of the Church (to which reference was made in the last lecture), had in some quarters been called in question.

The original form of the section had begun with the statement that " The Church of South India holds the faith which the Church has ever held in Jesus Christ, the Redeemer of the world, in whom men are saved by grace through faith: and in accordance with the revelation of God which He made, it worships one God in Trinity and Trinity in Unity." Statements followed that the Church of South India " accepts the Holy Scriptures of the Old and New Testaments as containing all things necessary to salvation and as the ultimate standard of faith ", and that " It also accepts the Apostles' Creed and the Creed commonly called Nicene as witnessing to and safeguarding that faith and as containing a sufficient statement thereof for a basis of union ". The section in this form presented no difficulty to Anglicans, and was declared in the

74

Report of the Derby Committee to be "un-exceptionable".

The altered form of the section, which had given rise to disquiet in the minds of some Anglicans, had been introduced at the instance of members of the Basel Mission who desired: (1) to give more emphatic primacy to the Scriptural "Word" as the supreme and decisive standard of faith, (2) to give greater and clearer emphasis to the Trinitarian revelation of God, and (3) to guard against Hindu theosophical syncretism, with its belief in a plurality of incarnations or "avatars" of the Divine, by declaring strongly that Christ, as the second Person of the Trinity, is "the incarnate Son of God", and as such "the Redeemer of the world".

The new form was as follows:

The Church of South India accepts the Holy Scriptures of the Old and New Testaments as containing all things necessary to salvation and as the supreme and decisive standard of faith: and acknowledges that the Church must always be ready to correct and reform itself in accordance with the teaching of those Scriptures as the Holy Spirit shall reveal it.

It also accepts the Apostles' Creed and the Creed commonly called the Nicene, as witnessing to and safeguarding that faith: and it thankfully acknowledges that same faith to be continuously confirmed by the Holy Spirit in the experience of the Church of Christ.

Thus it believes in God, the Father, the Creator of all things, by whose love we are preserved;

It believes in Jesus Christ, the incarnate Son of God and Redeemer of the world, in whom alone we are saved by grace, being justified from our sins by faith in Him;

It believes in the Holy Spirit, by whom we are sanctified and built up in Christ and in the fellowship of His Body;

And in this faith it worships the Father, Son and Holy Spirit, one God in Trinity and Trinity in Unity.

The Church of South India is competent to issue supplementary statements concerning the faith for the guidance of its teachers and the edification of the faithful, provided that such statements are not contrary to the truths of our religion revealed in the Holy Scriptures.[1]

It would be difficult to point to anything heretical in this revised form of the statement. Those who

---

[1] *Constitution of the Church of South India*, II. 5.

criticised it, however, regretted the alteration in the order of the paragraphs and the disappearance of the bold opening sentence declaring explicitly that " The Church of South India holds the faith which the Church has ever held ".   The suggestion was further made that the statement of Trinitarianism beginning " Thus it believes in God, the Father, the Creator of the world " and ending " in this faith it worships the Father, Son and Holy Spirit, one God in Trinity and Trinity in Unity ", could be read as " a kind of paraphrase of, or gloss upon, the Creed, which by omitting explicit reference to the historic facts affirmed therein could be taken to imply that they are regarded as unimportant ".[1] Particular trouble and misunderstanding was caused by a footnote to the form of the section appearing in the Basis of Union (though not repeated in the corresponding section of the Constitution of the Church), in which it was laid down that: " The uniting Churches accept the fundamental truths embodied in the Creeds . . . as providing a sufficient basis of union; but do not intend thereby to demand the assent of individuals to every word or phrase in them, or to exclude reasonable liberty of interpretation, or to assert that those Creeds are a complete expression of the Christian faith".   By

[1] *Derby Report*, p. 19.

this footnote (it was argued by those who were
disturbed by it) the door was opened to the kind
of " Modernism " which is prepared to play fast
and loose with the historical foundations of the
faith.   In vain was it argued that (in the words of
Bishop Newbigin):

> " To insist that reasonable liberty of interpre-
> tation be safeguarded is not to destroy the
> power of the Church to confess the faith, but
> to safeguard the condition of its so doing ",
> and that when the uniting Churches " claim
> that they do not intend to exclude reason-
> able liberty, it is implied that they have the
> power and intention to exclude unreasonable
> liberty ".[1]

The situation was complicated by the facts that
in the Church of England itself this particular
controversy was familiar, and that the members
of the Archbishops' Commission on Doctrine
(of which the late Archbishop Temple had been
chairman), reporting in 1937, had used words
which no official organ of the Church's corporate
mind would be at all likely to repudiate, but which
were regarded by not a few of the Church's more

[1] Newbigin, *op. cit.*, p. 142.

rigidly orthodox members as being dangerously liberal.[1]

Controversialists hostile to the South Indian Church made the most of their opportunity. The idea was sedulously fostered in many Anglican minds that there was some sinister motive behind the changed statement regarding the Faith of the Church, and that the leaders of the South Indian Church were deliberately opening the door to the entrance of heresy. Why, it was asked, was the recitation of the Creeds in worship not made compulsory in the new Church? If a congregation decided that it could not conscientiously recite the œcumenical Creed, was not the inference justified that it did not hold the true Catholic Faith? The wise provision of the South Indian Church Constitution, which, after giving the reasons for using the Creeds in worship, proceeded to enjoin that " in the ordinary congregational worship of any congregation, no authority of the Church of South India shall forbid the use of the Creeds or impose it against the will of the congregation " was not understood. No allowance was made by the Anglican critics for the inherited prejudice of those who had been traditionally brought up to object to

[1] See the Report, published under the title *Doctrine in the Church of England* (S.P.C.K., 1948), pp. 37 *sq.* and 81 *sqq.*

the use of Creeds on the ground of their being "man-made formulæ", and the objection to the use of the Creeds as formulæ was wrongly assumed to imply the denial of their substance.[1]

Despite all this argumentation, and the atmosphere of controversy in which the whole matter had by this time become unhappily involved, the members of the Lambeth Conference Committee who had had the opportunity of meeting the two South Indian bishops were left with no doubt in their minds of the orthodox intentions of the Church of South India, though by many of them the altered form of the statements regarding the Faith of the Church was still, doubtless, regretted. It may be added that assurances have since been officially given by the Theological Committee of the Church of South India and endorsed by its Synod, which include the categorical statement that the liberty of interpretation which by the footnote included in the Basis of Union the Church had desired to safeguard was not intended to extend to any denial of the substance of the historic faith of the Church. In the light of these

[1] See for the above the Open Letter to the Archbishop of Canterbury issued in 1943 by the Superiors of Certain Religious Communities under the title *The Unity of the Faith*, pp. 5–6, and in reply Bishop E. J. Palmer, *South India : The Meaning of the Scheme*, pp. 9–10.

assurances, the Joint Committees of the Convocations of Canterbury and York in their recent
unanimous Report on the Church of South India
were able to declare themselves " fully satisfied as
to the credal orthodoxy of the Church of South
India ".[1]

The Lambeth Conference Committee of 1948
achieved unanimity over the greater part of the
field. It was able to recommend to the full Conference a resolution (which the Conference duly
endorsed) giving thanks to God for the measure of
unity locally achieved in South India and pledging
its members to pray and work for its development
into an ever more perfect fulfilment of the will of
God for His Church, and looking forward hopefully
and with longing to the day when there should be
full communion between the Church of South India
and the Churches of the Anglican Communion.
It was able to recommend, in the sphere of immediate
and practical action, that former Anglicans, clerical
or lay, who were now members of the Church of
South India should (subject to the regulations of
responsible authority in the area concerned) be
accepted and allowed full privileges of ministry and

[1] *The Church of South India : Being the United Report
of the Joint Committees of the Convocations of Canterbury and
York,* p. 9.

communion in Anglican Churches: that Anglicans, clerical or lay, who might go to South India should not be subject to censure if they joined the Church of South India or took work in it, or if, when on a visit there, they accepted that Church's hospitality for the performance of priestly functions or the receiving of Holy Communion (subject, of course, to any regulations of the Churches, Provinces, or Dioceses to which they belonged): that episcopally confirmed lay communicants of the Church of South India should, subject to the approval of responsible authority, be received as communicants in Anglican Churches, though without thereby acquiring any new status or rights in relation to the Anglican Communion as a whole: and that other recognised South Indian communicants might, subject to the approval of authority and to any local regulation, be admitted to communion by an exercise of the principle of " economy ".

The Conference at the same time drew attention (as has already been noted) to the six points specified in the Report of its Committee on Unity and derived from the Derby Report, and expressed the hope that " so soon as it might appear to the authorities of the Church of South India to be expedient to take up the matter, such provisions of the Constitution of that Church and such statements contained therein as are known to have given rise either to uncertainty or to grave anxiety in the minds of many " might be " reconsidered with a view to their amendment ".

On one point—and on one point only—the Conference, led by its Committee, was constrained to acknowledge and register divergence of view. It was agreed unanimously that ministers of the Church of South India who had not been episcopally ordained should not be regarded as having acquired any new rights or status in relation to the Anglican Communion as a whole solely by reason of the fact that they were ministers of that Church. In regard, however, to the bishops, presbyters, and deacons consecrated or ordained in the Church of South India at or after the inauguration of that Church, the Conference was not able to make one recommendation agreed to by all.   It recorded the two following views, namely:

(1) a " majority " view, according to which such bishops, presbyters, and deacons should be acknowledged as true bishops, presbyters, and deacons in the Church of Christ and (subject only to such regulations as are normally made in such cases) should be accepted as such in every part of the Anglican Communion; and

(2) another view (held by a substantial minority), according to which it was not yet possible to pass any definite judgment upon the precise status of such bishops, presbyters, and deacons in the Church of Christ or to recommend that they be accepted in the Anglican Communion as bishops, presbyters, or deacons.

At the same time it was recorded that no member of the Conference desired to condemn outright, or to declare invalid, the episcopally consecrated and ordained ministry of the Church of South India. It was recognised that there would be differences of attitude in various parts of the Anglican Communion on this matter, and the unanimous hope was expressed that such differences might never in any part of the Anglican Communion be made a ground for condemnation of action taken by any Church, Province, or Diocese.

At the Lambeth Conference itself the theological grounds for this recorded divergence of view were not closely argued. The Report of the Committee by which the matter was considered included a paragraph as follows:

It is not difficult to declare that the orders and ministry of the Church of South India are regular and valid so far as regularity and validity can be guaranteed by the " form and matter " used in consecrating and ordaining. The Church of South India has been most careful to maintain the episcopal succession by the participation of three Anglican Bishops in its first consecration. Its declared intention is that in all future consecrations at least three bishops standing in the historic succession shall take part. It has used for the consecration of its bishops a form, and has prepared an ordinal, so similar in all essentials to those in use in the Anglican Communion that any suggestion that these forms were in themselves inadequate to convey the authority of the episcopate and the priesthood can be dismissed without question. But it remains true that form and manner alone are not sufficient to guarantee the character of a ministry. That can be substantiated only by the faith and practice of the Church itself.[1]

It was added on the following page of the Report that the minority held that there had not yet been " time in their judgment for the fruits of the union to be fully experienced and for the character of the Church of South India in its new corporate life to become apparent ". They were " of the opinion

[1] *Lambeth Conference 1948*, Part II, p. 47.

that time must be allowed for that Church to grow into fuller unity and to manifest its stability and its validity as a living part of the body of Christ ".[1]

Events in South India have moved rapidly. The Lambeth Conference Committee, in its whole consideration and treatment of the problem, had thought of the ministers and members of the Church of South India as falling neatly into categories—former Anglicans, former ministers and members of the South India United Church and of the Methodist Church, and newly consecrated or ordained bishops and presbyters and newly confirmed lay communicants: or again, as ex-Anglicans, ex-Congregationalists, ex-Methodists, and ex-Presbyterians. There was to be a process of " growing together ", but of course that would take time. And it is in fact inevitably true that the process of fully and completely growing together into the corporate life of what is now a single unified Church will take time, and that it would be absurd either to suppose or to claim that it has been already completely accomplished. Nevertheless, those who have visited the Church of South India since its unification agree in testifying to the immense difference which unification has already made. It is said that in January 1950 when the

[1] *Lambeth Conference 1948*, Part II, p. 48.

new Metropolitan of India (the Most Rev. A. N. Mukerjee, then Bishop of Delhi) visited South India in order to present to its Synod the Resolutions of the General Council and Episcopal Synod of the Church of India, Burma, and Ceylon (the first Church of our Communion to accept formally the Lambeth " majority " view), he went expecting to find a composite Church Synod, the members of which would still readily fall into discernible groups of ex-Anglicans, ex-Congregationalists, ex-Methodists, and ex-Presbyterians. He was immensely impressed (and his point of view is believed to have been substantially changed) by the fact that, in the discussions at which he was present, it was seldom possible to judge, from the speeches made, what had been the earlier ecclesiastical allegiance or affiliation of the speakers. So, too, there is a story (for which there is excellent authority) that at a recent discussion between South Indian Churchmen and Lutherans, an ex-Congregationalist (now a member of the Church of South India) who at an earlier stage, before the union, had been among the stoutest oppponents of episcopacy, was heard to say to one of the Lutheran theologians—" Of course you must realise there is one principle which the Church of South India will never give up, and that is its insistence upon the historic episcopate!"

A third story is that of the ex-Congregationalist Indian woman coming away from a solemn Eucharist in Bangalore Cathedral with her eyes filled with tears, and remarking: " To think that this beautiful worship now belongs to *us*! "

The Joint Committees of the Convocations of Canterbury and York which produced the Convocation Report on *The Church of South India* had had contact at second hand with South India through the visit of their chairman, the Bishop of Chichester, to confer personally with the authorities of the Church of South India in South India itself. They were alive to the growing unity of the South Indian Church and to its own desire to be dealt with not as a congeries of formerly distinct denominational groups, but in its corporate unity as a Church. For Anglican purposes it was impossible to refrain from continuing to make a distinction in status between those ministers who had, and those who had not, been episcopally ordained. But the joint Committees in the eighth of the series of resolutions which they proposed (all of which were in the sequel accepted by both Houses of both Convocations) no longer followed the Lambeth Conference Report in recommending a difference of attitude towards bishops and presbyters consecrated or ordained before Union, and those consecrated or ordained at or since Union in South India, but provided that all the episcopally ordained South Indian clergy (whatever might be the decision in particular dioceses on their ministry) should be treated alike.

The Report (too long to be here summarised) is a published document, and should be read.[1] It contains valuable appendices, including both the Interim Reply of the Theological Committee of the South Indian Church to the six questions mentioned in the Report of the Lambeth Conference, and also the replies officially given to the questions addressed to the Church of South India, through its Moderator, by the Joint Committees of the two Convocations. Both series of questions in effect followed the same lines, and the Report chronicles the fact that the Convocation Committees regarded the answers respecting the credal orthodoxy of the Church of South India and those concerning the Sacraments, Confirmation, and Synodical Procedure, as a " satisfactory clarification of important points on which anxiety had been expressed ".[2] The replies to the two other questions, which were concerned (*a*) with the continuance of relations

[1] It can be obtained from the Church Information Board for half a crown.

[2] *The Church of South India*, p. 9.

of intercommunion with non-episcopal Churches, and (*b*) with the continued possibility of the admission of non-episcopally ordained ministers into the Church, inevitably caused rather more difficulty in many Anglican minds. The Church of South India was obliged to explain that in no reasonably foreseeable circumstances would the Church of South India break off relationship with those parent Churches with which it now enjoys unrestricted fellowship; and that, on the continued possibility of the occasional admission of non-episcopally ordained ministers into the Church, the decision to be taken in unforeseeable circumstances at the end of the thirty years' period could not now be anticipated.

The policy which, in the light of all this, was recommended to and accepted by the two Convocations laid it down: (1) that all clergy of the Church of South India, without discrimination, may at the discretion of the bishop be invited to preach in Anglican pulpits in England: (2) that former Anglican clergy who are now ministers of the Church of South India may in England, if desirous of doing so, and subject to normal legal requirements, be allowed either permanently or temporarily to revert to their former Anglican status: (3) that former Anglican communicants who now belong to the Church of South India may receive Holy Communion in the Church of England and that other communicant members of the Church of South India may at the bishop's discretion be welcomed as visitors: (4) that members of the Church of England visiting South India may accept the hospitality of the Church there for the performing of priestly functions or the receiving of Holy Communion: and (5) that, pending the taking of further order by the Church, the bishop of a diocese may at his discretion allow or not allow a South Indian bishop or presbyter episcopally consecrated or ordained before, at, or after, the Union to celebrate the Holy Communion in a church by invitation of the incumbent, it being understood by all concerned that in view of the conditions of Church life in England any one accepting such permission will for the present celebrate only in churches under the jurisdiction of the bishops of the Provinces of Canterbury and York.[1]

The discretion conceded by this last resolution to individual bishops to act, according to their own judgment, either upon the Lambeth " minor-

[1] The precise text of the Resolutions passed by the Convocations is conveniently accessible in the United Report of their Joint Committees, *The Church of South India*, pp. 25 *sqq.*

ity " or upon the Lambeth " majority " view of the
South Indian ministry reflects a division of opinion
in the English Convocations corresponding to the
division of opinion among the bishops at Lambeth.
The Provinces of Canterbury and York, deciding
for the present not to press the matter to a decision
by majority vote, have postponed for a period of
five years the expression of any official or corporate judgment on the South Indian ministry, in
the hope that by the end of that time the mind of
the Church may have become clearer.

The Convocation Report, however, did what the
Lambeth Conference did not do—it set forth a
statement of the grounds upon which the upholders
respectively of the " majority " and of the
" minority " views based their positions.[1] The
statement of the " majority " view appears to me
to be convincing, and to state without rhetoric the
theological and practical arguments that ought to
be weighed: I need not do more with regard to it
than say simply that I endorse it. The statement
of the " minority " view I shall venture to criticise.
It contains three paragraphs, of which the first
deals with the problems raised for Anglicans by
the initial admission of non-episcopally ordained

[1] Convocation Report on *The Church of South India*, pp.
12–17.

ministers to the functions and status of presbyters on a level with those who have received ordination at the hands of a bishop, and the impossibility of any definite assurance being given that the occasional admission of non-episcopally ordained ministers into the Church would be excluded even after the expiration of the thirty years' period. The paragraph is somewhat rhetorically expressed, and the scale upon which the latter problem is likely to arise may be thought to be exaggerated. No attention is paid, for example, to the information, supplied from India, that—

for practical purposes this question only concerns foreign missionaries coming to serve in C.S.I. These at present constitute less than five per cent of the ministry of the Church. Their number is decreasing. Moreover, some of the societies concerned are adopting the policy of sending out their men unordained to be ordained in C.S.I. The number of ministers who have not received episcopal ordination received into the permanent ministry of the Church is likely to be small.[1]

It is said that initially the proportion of non-episcopally ordained ministers to those episcopally

[1] *Op. cit.*, p. 48.

ordained in the Church of South India was about
fifty per cent. Already the balance is altering, since,
of course, all ordinations are now episcopal, and it
is said that about 150 new ministers have been
ordained since the Union took place. It is to be
remembered further that all ministers serving in the
Church of South India have declared their acceptance of the constitution of an episcopal Church,
and are working under the authority of bishops, to
whom they have acknowledged allegiance as to
their fathers in God. It is also right to take into
account the past history of Anglicanism. There
are examples known to historians of ministers
coming from foreign Churches who appear to have
been admitted (however irregularly) into Anglican
benefices in the post-Reformation era without having
first been episcopally ordained.[1] Of greater importance are the facts (sometimes conveniently forgotten) that the present Episcopal Church in Scotland derives its episcopal succession through the
episcopate which was restored in Scotland from
England in 1662, and that the bishops then consecrated for Scotland inaugurated their episcopate
by the acceptance of presbyterian ministers as

[1] See the discussion in *The Apostolic Ministry*, Essay
VII (1), in which the known instances are considered, and
their significance minimised.

parish priests. The Church of England is not being asked to accept for itself the regulations and policy of the Church of South India, but only to refuse to regard them as constituting a fatal barrier to the acceptance by Anglicans of the ministry of such ministers of the Church of South India as have been episcopally ordained. It is complained, in the statement in the Convocation Report of the " minority " view, that " behind these provisions and negotiations there is implicit a wholly novel doctrine of the ministry, and indeed of the necessity (or otherwise) of episcopal ordination, never yet held by any Christian body which could fairly be called ' part of the one, holy, catholic and apostolic Church ' ". It is difficult to see on what grounds the implied doctrine—presumably the doctrine that episcopal ordination is not in all circumstances the indispensable pre-requisite of a valid ministry—can be described as " wholly novel ", for it has in fact been maintained in large areas of Christendom for centuries. If what is meant is simply that the Roman Catholic and Orthodox Churches would not endorse such a view, and that the Anglican Church (though with a divided mind on the subject) would not officially endorse it, the point is surely so obvious as to be hardly worth making. The Anglican Church is in any case not being asked to accept *for itself* the doctrine in question. The implicit denial, however, (if such be intended) that Churches which do not consider episcopal ordination to be a *sine qua non* of a valid ministry can yet be in a true sense parts of " the one, holy, catholic, and apostolic Church " would be repudiated by large numbers of Anglican theologians, and the inclusion of the sentence criticised in a document which, in view of its character and scope, could not fail to be widely read by non-Anglicans, including members of the Reformed and Lutheran Churches in many lands, must be described as unfortunate.

The second paragraph in the Convocation Report statement of the " minority " view makes the point that the South Indian Church, though itself in process of becoming fully episcopal, intends to continue to be in communion with the non-episcopal Churches from which some fifty per cent of its initial membership was derived. This, it is urged, implies logically the doctrine that " there is no theological objection to full intercommunion between episcopal and non-episcopal bodies ",[1] a doctrine which (though it has been not infrequently held and acted upon, as a matter of historical fact,

[1] Convocation Report on *The Church of South India*, p. 16.

by individual Anglicans) has never been endorsed or accepted officially by the Church of England, which indeed has stood and still stands in its own practice for the contrary view. Can it not continue to do so? The statement in the Convocation Report of the " majority " view, anticipating this particular objection, observes not unreasonably that—

> the fact that the Church of South India, though itself committed to episcopacy, does not refuse to be in communion with non-episcopal Churches need not oblige Anglican Churches, as a condition of closer fellowship, to adopt a like view. They would remain free to continue to bear their traditional witness by themselves entering into relations of full communion only with fully episcopal Churches.

The argument put forward in the " minority " statement—that the freedom of intercommunion with non-episcopalians to which the Church of South India is committed " seems wholly to ignore the scriptural and patristic conception of the Eucharist as the sacrament of corporate unity in the Church, the Body of Christ " (apparently on the ground that it " sets the individual free to participate in the sacrament without recognising any duty of allegiance to the community which administers it ")—would appear, if accepted, to rule out all forms of intercommunion between Churches not holding identical doctrines. But the Church of England, as the upholders of the " majority " view point out, is committed by a concordat to the practice of intercommunion with the Old Catholic Churches on the basis of the acknowledgment on both sides that " Intercommunion does not require from either Communion the acceptance of all doctrinal opinion, sacramental devotion, or liturgical practice, characteristic of the other, but implies that each believes the other to hold all the essentials of the Christian faith ".

The arguments in the two " minority " paragraphs just criticised are alleged as grounds for the suspension of judgment on the South Indian ministry. It is admitted that in the Church of South India a true succession of ministerial commission through the episcopate has been preserved, and that the orders and ministry of the Church of South India are " regular and valid so far as regularity and validity can be guaranteed by the ' form and manner ' used in consecrating and ordaining ".[1] A minister of the South Indian Church, thus ordained, may be imagined as asking " What

[1] *Lambeth Conference 1948*, Part II, p. 47.

lack I yet?" It is to be remembered that the orders of the Anglican Church itself are not undisputed. The Roman Catholic Church disallows them partly at least on the ground of defect of intention, alleging that for valid orders there must be an explicit intention on the part of the Church to ordain priests capable of offering the eucharistic sacrifice as understood by the Church of Rome. There are Anglican quarters in which a defect of intention, more or less of this kind, has been alleged against the orders of the Church of South India. In the statement of the " minority " view put forward in the Convocation Report this particular argument does not appear, and the " majority " contention seems to have been tacitly accepted that, so far as intention is concerned, it suffices that the Church of South India should have the intention of " doing what the Church does ", and of continuing by means of its consecrations and ordinations the full ministry of the Word and Sacraments in accordance with the mind of Christ.

The orders and ministry of the Church of England are, however, in practice disallowed not only by Roman Catholics but by the Orthodox Churches as well: and the attitude of the " minority " Anglicans towards the orders and ministry of the

Church of South India is disturbingly similar to
that of the Orthodox Churches towards those of
the Church of England. Technically valid, or
possibly valid, orders (so the argument runs) may
not be reckoned for righteousness to a Church
which possesses them unless that Church concurs
wholly in doctrine and practice with the Church
which is in effect sitting in judgment upon it. The
Anglican Communion (I would submit), having
concluded a concordat upon different lines with the
Old Catholics, is debarred now from taking up
quite this attitude, even though it be freely admitted
that, for the purposes of intercommunion, the
possession of valid orders by a sister Church is by
itself not enough; there must be also some assurance of orthodoxy; and it is not, therefore, without
importance that the credal orthodoxy of the South
Indian Church has been now officially acknowledged.

There are, in effect, two small indications which,
if the argument is to be pressed, might be held to
suggest that, in respect of the doctrine of Holy
Orders and of the question of validity, the upholders of the " majority " position are in process
of gaining the victory. In the Resolution, passed
by the Convocations—which allows discretion to
individual bishops (pending the taking of further

order by the Church) to permit episcopally ordained South Indian presbyters to celebrate Holy Communion in parish Churches—a position has been taken up which is in effect incompatible with any eventual decision involving the theory that they are inherently incapable of being the ministers of a valid sacrament; and in the same Resolution (as has already been pointed out) there has been no distinction drawn between bishops and presbyters consecrated or ordained at or since union and those previously consecrated or ordained in the Anglican fold. The contention of the " majority " that between ministers consecrated or ordained in almost exactly the same way and by bishops standing in the same episcopal succession and now ministering side by side in the same Church there is no distinction to be drawn on theological grounds, has here also been tacitly admitted. If in particular English dioceses South Indian clergy should, by an exercise of the bishop's discretion, be excluded from celebrating Holy Communion, the grounds of such exclusion would in effect have to be no longer hesitation about their orders, but dubiety, in the mind of the bishop concerned, of the sufficient catholicity of the Church to which they belong.

The official mind of the Church of England,

expressed through the utterances alike of its
bishops at Lambeth and of its Convocations (including the Houses of Clergy) since Lambeth,
looks forward with hope and prayer to the day
when full communion may be possible between
the Church of South India and the Church of
England. To that end it is of obvious importance
that the full riches of the Catholic inheritance of the
Anglican Church should, so far as may be practicable, be poured into the South Indian Church.
There are "minority" Anglicans, the rigidity of
whose doctrinal position would make it genuinely
difficult—perhaps impossible—for them to accept
work, or to serve personally, in the Church of
South India; though it is important to recognise
that there are ex-Anglicans, formerly Anglo-
Catholics, of a less rigid sort, who, without appre-
ciably changing either their theology or their
ecclesiastical practice, have found themselves able
to do so. From the point of view of ecclesiastical
statesmanship it is essential that in South India the
witness of Anglicanism of the more "Catholic"
type should not be allowed to die out, but that on
the contrary it should, under the conditions of
freedom allowed by the South Indian Church,
continue to make itself felt and to help forward the
development of the "degree of catholicity" which

the Church of South India has " already attained ".[1]
" There is no need ", say the authors of the recent
Convocation Report, " to stress the urgent need
in which the Church of South India stands, and
will increasingly stand, of all the help which the
Church of England can provide. . . . We are convinced that it is the bounden duty of members of
the Church of England to provide ", either by
offers of personal service or by gifts of money,
" such support as, in conscience, they feel able to
give".[2]

[1] *Lambeth Conference 1948*, Part II, p. 46.
[2] Convocation Report on *The Church of South India*,
p. 24.

APPENDIX I

AN EXPERIMENTAL LITURGY

THE Church of South India allows in its public worship freedom for any or each of its congregations either to use historic forms or not to do so: and its Constitution contains a proviso regulating the procedure to be followed whenever in any particular congregation a new or hitherto unaccustomed order of worship is introduced. Subject to this proviso, the Synod of the Church, at its second meeting (held at Madras in January 1950) gave provisional authorisation for the use, under diocesan sanction, of the Liturgy here printed, the copyright of which belongs to the Church of South India. The permission generously given by the Synod Liturgy Committee of C.S.I. for the inclusion here of the Order of Service thus authorised is most gratefully acknowledged.

THE SERVICE OF THE LORD'S SUPPER
OR
The Holy Eucharist

THE PREPARATION

*As the ministers come to the Lord's Table, the people
shall stand.*

*A hymn or psalm, or part thereof, may be sung or
said.*

The presbyter shall say, the people standing :

Let us pray.

ALMIGHTY God, unto whom all hearts be
open, all desires known, and from whom no
secrets are hid; Cleanse the thoughts of our hearts
by the inspiration of thy Holy Spirit, that we may
perfectly love thee, and worthily magnify thy holy
name; through Jesus Christ our Lord. **Amen.**

¶ *Then all shall sing or say :*

**GLORY to God in the highest, and on earth
peace among men in whom is his good pleasure. We praise thee, we bless thee, we worship thee, we glorify thee, we give thanks to
thee for thy great glory, O Lord God, Heavenly
King, God the Father Almighty.**

O Lord the only-begotten Son Jesus Christ,

O Lord God, Lamb of God, Son of the Father, that takest away the sin of the world, have mercy upon us; thou that takest away the sin of the world, receive our prayer. Thou that sittest at the right hand of God the Father, have mercy upon us.

For thou only art Holy, thou only art Lord, thou only art Most High, O Jesu Christ, with the Holy Ghost, in the glory of God the Father. Amen.

¶ *Or another hymn or lyric may be sung.*

¶ *Or this ancient hymn may be said or sung, and thrice repeated :*

Holy God.

Holy and Mighty, Holy and Immortal, have mercy on us.

Or this litany may be used, the deacon leading the responses :

WORTHY is the Lamb that hath been slain to receive the power, and riches, and wisdom, and might, and honour, and glory, and blessing.

Unto the Lamb be glory !

Unto him that sitteth on the throne, and unto the Lamb, be the blessing, and the honour, and the glory, and the dominion, for ever and ever.

Unto the Lamb be glory !

Worthy art thou, for thou wast slain, and didst purchase unto God with thy blood men of every tribe, and tongue, and people, and nation.

Unto the Lamb be glory! Salvation unto our God which sitteth on the throne, and unto the Lamb. Blessing and glory, and wisdom, and thanksgiving, and honour, and power, and might, be unto our God for ever and ever. Amen.

Then shall the presbyter say :

BELOVED, hear what Saint Paul says to those who would draw near to the Lord's Table.

For I received of the Lord that which also I delivered unto you, how that the Lord Jesus in the night in which he was betrayed took bread; and when he had given thanks, he brake it, and said, This is my body, which is for you: this do in remembrance of me. In like manner also the cup, after supper, saying, This cup is the new covenant in my blood: this do, as oft as ye drink it, in remembrance of me. For as often as ye eat this bread, and drink the cup, ye proclaim the Lord's death till he come. Wherefore whosoever shall eat the bread or drink the cup of the Lord unworthily, shall be guilty of the body and the blood of the Lord. But let a man prove himself, and so let him eat of the bread, and drink of the cup. For he that eateth or drinketh, eateth and drinketh judgement unto himself, if he discern not the body.

The Ten Commandments, or our Lord's summary of the Law, may be read here, the people responding at the end :

Lord, have mercy upon us, and incline our hearts to keep this law.

If the Ten Commandments be used, the people may so respond after each Commandment till the last, and then :

Lord, have mercy upon us, and write all these thy laws in our hearts, we beseech thee.

¶ *If no service of preparation has been previously held, this exhortation may be said by the presbyter :*

DEARLY beloved, it is right that we who would come to the communion of our Lord Jesus Christ, in which he truly gives unto us his Body and Blood as food and drink of everlasting life for the strengthening of our faith, should take to heart the mystery of the Lord's Table. The mystery is this: The Good Shepherd has laid down his life for the sheep; he who was without guile has died for sinners, the Head for his members, the Bridegroom for his bride the Church; in obedience to the Father's will and in infinite love to us, the High Priest has offered himself as the perfect sacrifice. And thus by his death he has done away with all that stood in the way of our fellowship with God the Father, that we may assuredly be his children, be upheld by his love, be guided by him all the days of our life, and rejoice in the hope of his glory. As our Lord thus offers to us the fellowship of his Spirit, so he seeks to change us into his image. He pours his love into our hearts that we may learn to love him, to love one another, and also to love our enemies. In the power of his resurrection he wants us to crucify the old man with his lusts, and to walk in newness of life. In the fellowship of his sufferings he wants us to bear trials and tribulations patiently, to the glory of his name.

Any who will not lay to heart or obey these words, but are minded to continue in sin and unrighteousness, let them not approach the Table of the Lord here spread for the Church which is his Body. Let a man examine himself, and so let him eat of that bread and drink of that cup. The worthiness which the Lord requires from us is that we be truly sorry for our sins, and find our joy and salvation in him. For we come to the Supper not as righteous in ourselves, but trusting in the righteousness of Christ our Saviour, acknow-

ledging that we are in the midst of death. United
with him who is holy, even our Lord Jesus Christ,
we are accepted by the Father and invited to partake
of this holy meal.

¶ *Or the following may be used instead :*

YE that do truly and earnestly repent you of your
sins, and are in love and charity with your neigh-
bours, and intend to live a new life, following
the commandments of God, and walking from
henceforth in his holy ways; Draw near with faith,
and take this Holy Sacrament to your comfort;
and make your humble confession to Almighty
God, meekly kneeling upon your knees.

*All shall kneel, and silence shall be kept for a space ;
then all shall confess their sins together.*

The presbyter shall say :

Let us humbly confess our sins to Almighty
God.

¶ *The deacon leading, all shall say together :*

HEAVENLY Father, we confess that we have
sinned against thee and our neighbour. We
have called evil good and good evil; we have
walked in darkness rather than in light; we
have named the name of Christ but have not
departed from iniquity. Have mercy upon us,
we beseech thee; for the sake of Jesus Christ,

forgive us all our sins; cleanse us, by thy Holy Spirit, from all defilement of flesh and spirit; and enable us heartily to forgive others, and to serve thee henceforth in newness of life, to the glory of thy holy name. Amen.

¶ *Or the presbyter may use certain other forms of confession.*

Then the presbyter shall stand and say :

HEAR the gracious words of God to all who truly turn to him through Jesus Christ.

Come unto me, all ye that labour and are heavy laden, and I will give you rest.

God so loved the world, that he gave his only-begotten Son, that whosoever believeth on him should not perish, but have eternal life.

Faithful is the saying, and worthy of all acceptation, that Jesus Christ came into the world to save sinners.

If any man sin, we have an Advocate with the Father, Jesus Christ the righteous: and he is the propitiation for our sins.

A short silence may be kept, and then the presbyter shall say :

ALMIGHTY God, our heavenly Father, who of his great mercy has promised forgiveness of sins to all who forgive their brethren and with hearty repentance and true faith turn unto him; Have mercy upon you; pardon and deliver you from all your sins; confirm and strengthen you in all goodness; and bring you to eternal life; through Jesus Christ our Lord.

Amen.   Thanks be to God.

This Declaration of God's Forgiveness may be used as a prayer, the presbyter saying ' us ' and ' our ' for ' you ' and ' your ';   if so, the prayer should precede the reading of the Gracious Words of God.

The Lord be with you.

And with thy spirit.

Let us pray.

Here shall follow the Collect of the Day, or another short prayer.

The reading of the Scripture shall follow, all standing.

After the lesson from the Old Testament, the people shall say :

Thanks be to thee, O God.

A psalm or a part thereof, or a hymn or lyric, may be sung.

After the Epistle, the people shall again say :

Thanks be to thee, O God.

But after the Gospel the people shall say :

Praise be to thee, O Christ.

Then the sermon shall be preached, the people sitting.

The sermon shall end with an ascription of praise to God, the people standing.

Then shall be said or sung by all :

I BELIEVE in one God the Father Almighty, Maker of heaven and earth, And of all things visible and invisible :

And in one Lord Jesus Christ, the only-begotten Son of God, Begotten of his Father before all worlds, God of God, Light of Light, Very God of very God, Begotten, not made, Being of one substance with the Father, By whom all things were made : Who for us men, and for our salvation came down from heaven, And was incarnate by the Holy Ghost of the Virgin Mary, And was made man, And was crucified also for us under Pontius Pilate. He suffered and was buried, And the third day he rose again according to the Scriptures, And ascended into heaven, And sitteth on the right hand of the Father. And he shall come again with glory to judge both the quick and the dead : Whose kingdom shall have no end.

And I believe in the Holy Ghost, The Lord, The Giver of life, Who proceedeth from the Father and the Son, Who with the Father and the Son together is worshipped and glorified, Who spake by the Prophets.

Appendix I

And I believe One, Holy, Catholic, and Apostolic Church. I acknowledge one Baptism for the remission of sins. And I look for the Resurrection of the dead, And the Life of the world to come. Amen.

The Apostles' Creed may be used instead.

A hymn may here be sung, followed by the announcements and by biddings for prayer.

Then all shall kneel, and, with the deacon leading, shall offer up their prayers for others as well as for themselves.

¶ *The following Litany may be used :*

Let us pray.

ALMIGHTY God, who hast taught us to make prayers and supplications, and to give thanks for all men; hear us when we pray : That it may please thee to inspire continually the universal Church with the spirit of truth, unity, and concord :

Hear us, we beseech thee.

That it may please thee to grant that all they that do confess thy holy name may agree in the truth of thy holy Word, and live in unity and godly love :

Hear us, we beseech thee.

That it may please thee to lead all nations in the paths of righteousness and peace :

Hear us, we beseech thee.

115

That it may please thee to direct all kings and rulers, especially our rulers, that under them we and all men may be godly and quietly governed:

Hear us, we beseech thee.

That it may please thee to give grace to all bishops, presbyters, and deacons, especially thy servant (*naming the bishop of the diocese*), that by their life and doctrine they may set forth thy true and living Word, and rightly and duly administer thy holy Sacraments:

Hear us, we beseech thee.

That it may please thee to guide and prosper all those who are labouring for the spread of thy Gospel among the nations, and to enlighten with thy Spirit all places of education, learning, and healing:

Hear us, we beseech thee.

That it may please thee that through thy heavenly benediction we may be saved from dearth and famine, and may with thankful hearts enjoy the fruits of the earth in their season:

Hear us, we beseech thee.

That it may please thee to give to all thy people thy heavenly grace; and specially to this congregation here present; that, with meek heart and due reverence, they may hear, and receive thy holy Word; truly serving thee in holiness and righteousness all the days of their life:

Hear us, we beseech thee.

That it may please thee of thy goodness, O Lord, to comfort and succour all them, who in this transitory life are in trouble, sorrow, need, sickness, or any other adversity:

Hear us, we beseech thee.

And we praise thee for all thy servants departed this life in thy faith and fear, beseeching thee to give us grace that we may follow their good examples, and with them be made partakers of thy heavenly kingdom:

Hear us, we beseech thee.

Then the presbyter shall say :

Let us pray.

ALMIGHTY God, the fountain of all wisdom, who knowest our necessities before we ask, and our ignorance in asking; We beseech thee to have compassion upon our infirmities; and those things, which for our unworthiness we dare not, and for our blindness we cannot ask, vouchsafe to give us, for the worthiness of thy Son Jesus Christ our Lord. **Amen.**

¶ *Or this Litany may be used instead, the deacon leading :*

FOR the peace that is from above, and for the salvation of our souls, let us pray to the Lord.

Lord, have mercy (*or*, **Lord, hear our prayer;** *and so throughout*).

For the peace of the whole world, for the welfare of God's holy Churches, and for the union of all, let us pray to the Lord.

Lord, have mercy.

For our bishops and all other ministers, for their succour, maintenance, peace, health, and salvation, and for the work of their hands, let us pray to the Lord.

Lord, have mercy.

For the rulers of our country and for all in authority, let us pray to the Lord.

Lord, have mercy.

Thanking God for all his servants who have served him here and are now at rest, that we may with them enter into the fulness of his unending joy, let us pray to the Lord.

Lord, have mercy.

For ourselves and for all who call upon the name of Christ, that he may remake us in his own image, let us pray to the Lord.

Lord, have mercy.

Then the presbyter shall say :

Let us pray.

ALMIGHTY God, the fountain of all wisdom,

who knowest our necessities before we ask, and our ignorance in asking; We beseech thee to have compassion upon our infirmities; and those things, which for our unworthiness we dare not, and for our blindness we cannot ask, vouchsafe to give us, for the worthiness of thy Son Jesus Christ our Lord. **Amen.**

¶ *Or the presbyter may use certain other forms.*

Then shall follow the Benediction :

The grace of our Lord Jesus Christ, the love of God, and the fellowship of the Holy Spirit, be with you all. **Amen.**

The excommunicate shall now leave the church. It is expected that all of communicant status will stay to partake of the Eucharist.

THE BREAKING OF THE BREAD

All shall stand for the Offertory, and the presbyter shall say :

Behold, how good and joyful a thing it is, brethren, to dwell together in unity.

We who are many are one bread, one body, for we all partake of the one bread.

I will offer in his dwelling an oblation with great gladness, I will sing and speak praises unto the Lord.

The ' Peace ' may be given here.

The bread and wine for the Communion, together with the gifts of the people, are now placed on the Table. A hymn may meanwhile be sung.
All shall kneel, and the presbyter shall say :

Let us pray.

HOLY Father, who through the blood of thy dear Son hast consecrated for us a new and living way to thy throne of grace, we humbly beseech thee to take and use these gifts for thy glory. All that is in the heaven and earth is thine, and of thine own do we give to thee. Mercifully accept us as with all these gifts we dedicate ourselves, unworthy as we are, to thy service, through Jesus Christ our Lord. **Amen.**

The following prayer may be said by the presbyter alone, or by all together :

BE present, be present, O Jesus, thou good High Priest, as thou wast in the midst of thy disciples, and make thyself known to us in the breaking of the bread, who livest and reignest with the Father and the Holy Spirit, one God, world without end. **Amen.**

The Lord be with you;
And with thy spirit.

Lift up your hearts;
We lift them up unto the Lord.

Let us give thanks unto our Lord God;

It is meet and right so to do.

IT is verily meet, right, and our bounden duty, that we should at all times, and in all places, give thanks unto thee, O Holy Lord, Father Almighty, Everlasting God, through Jesus Christ thy Son our Lord, through whom thou didst create the heavens and the earth and all that in them is, and didst make man in thine own image, and thy tender mercies are over all thy works.

Therefore with angels and archangels and with all the company of heaven, we laud and magnify thy glorious name; evermore praising thee, and saying, Holy, Holy, Holy, Lord God of hosts, heaven and earth are full of thy glory. Glory be to thee, O Lord most high.

There may be added here,
Blessed be he that hath come and is to come in the name of the Lord, Hosanna in the highest.

Truly holy, truly blessed art thou, O heavenly Father, who of thy tender love towards mankind didst give thine only Son Jesus Christ to take our nature upon him and to suffer death upon the cross for our redemption; who made there, by his one oblation of himself once offered, a full, perfect, and sufficient sacrifice, oblation, and satisfaction, for the sins of the whole world; and did institute, and in his holy Gospel command us to continue, a perpetual memory of that his precious death, until his coming again: Who, in the same night that he was betrayed, took bread, and when he had given thanks, he brake it, and gave it to his disciples, saying, Take, eat, this is my body which is given for you: do this in remembrance of me. Likewise after supper he took the cup, and, when he had given thanks, he gave it to them, saying, Drink ye all of this; for this is my blood of the new covenant, which is shed for you and for many for the remission of sins: do this, as oft as ye shall drink it, in remembrance of me. **Amen.**

Thy death, O Lord, we commemorate, thy resurrection we confess, and thy second coming we await. Have mercy on us.

Wherefore, O Father, having in remembrance the precious death and passion, and glorious resurrection and ascension, of thy Son our Lord, we thy servants do this in remembrance of him, as he hath commanded, until he comes again, giving thanks to thee for the perfect redemption which thou hast wrought for us in him.

We give thanks to thee, we praise thee, we glorify thee, O Lord our God.

And we most humbly beseech thee, O merciful

Father, to sanctify with thy Holy Spirit, us and these thine own gifts of bread and wine, that the bread which we break may be the communion of the body of Christ, and the cup which we bless the communion of the blood of Christ. Grant that being joined together in him, we may all attain to the unity of the faith, and may grow up in all things unto him who is the Head, even Christ, our Lord, by whom and with whom, in the unity of the Holy Spirit, all honour and glory be unto thee, O Father Almighty, world without end. **Amen.**

As our Saviour Christ hath commanded and taught us, we are bold to say:

Our Father, which art in heaven, Hallowed by thy Name; Thy kingdom come; Thy will be done; In earth as it is in heaven. Give us this day our daily bread. And forgive us our trespasses, As we forgive them that trespass against us. And lead us not into temptation; But deliver us from evil: For thine is the kingdom, The power and the glory, For ever and ever. Amen.

Then shall silence be kept for a space, all kneeling.

WE do not presume to come to this Thy Table, O merciful Lord, trusting in our own righteousness, but in thy manifold and great mercies. We are not worthy so much as to gather up the crumbs under thy Table. But thou are the same Lord, whose property is always to have mercy: Grant us therefore, gracious Lord, so to eat the Flesh of thy dear Son Jesus Christ, and to drink his Blood, that our sinful bodies and souls may be made clean by his most precious Body and Blood, and that we may evermore dwell in him, and he in us. **Amen.**

Then the presbyter shall rise, and break the bread.

While he and those ministering with him receive the communion, the people may sing :

O Lamb of God, that takest away the sin of the world, have mercy upon us.

O Lamb of God, that takest away the sin of the world, have mercy upon us.

O Lamb of God, that takest away the sin of the world, grant us thy peace.

The communion shall then be administered to the people, in the place and manner customary in the congregation concerned.

It is suggested that the wine be administered from the cup with a spoon.

When all have partaken, they shall kneel, and the presbyter shall say :

Let us give thanks to God.

¶ *Then shall follow this prayer:*

O ALMIGHTY God, our heavenly Father, who hast accepted us as thy children in thy beloved Son Jesus Christ, our Lord, and hast fed us with the spiritual food of his most precious Body and Blood, giving us the forgiveness of our sins and the promise of everlasting life, we thank and praise thee for these inestimable benefits, and we offer and present unto thee ourselves, our souls and bodies, to be a holy and living sacrifice, which is our reasonable service. Grant us grace not to be conformed to this world, but to be transformed by the renewing of our minds, that we may learn what is thy good and perfect will, and so obey thee here on earth, that we may at the last rejoice with all thy saints in thy heavenly kingdom; through Jesus Christ our Lord, who liveth and reigneth with thee and the Holy Spirit, one God, for ever.

¶ *Or this :*

ALMIGHTY and everlasting God, we most heartily thank thee, for that thou dost vouchsafe to feed us, who have duly received these holy mysteries, with the spiritual food of the most precious Body and Blood of thy Son our Saviour Jesus Christ; and dost assure us thereby of thy favour and goodness towards us; and that we are very members incorporate in the mystical Body of thy

Son, which is the blessed company of all faithful people; and are also heirs through hope of thy everlasting kingdom, by the merits of the most precious death and passion of thy dear Son. Wherefore we offer and present unto thee ourselves, our souls and bodies, to be a reasonable, holy, and living sacrifice unto thee. And we most humbly beseech thee, O heavenly Father, so to assist us with thy grace, that we may continue in that holy fellowship, and do all such good works as thou hast prepared for us to walk in; through Jesus Christ our Lord, to whom, with thee and the Holy Ghost, be all honour and glory, world without end.

And all shall say :

Amen. Blessing, and glory, and wisdom, and thanksgiving, and honour, and power, and might, be unto our God for ever and ever. Amen.

The presbyter shall then give the Blessing.

THE peace of God, which passeth all understanding, keep your hearts and minds in the knowledge and love of God, and of his Son Jesus Christ our Lord: and the blessing of God Almighty, the Father, the Son, and the Holy Ghost, be amongst you and remain with you always. **Amen.**

A hymn of praise and thanksgiving, or Psalm 103,

Appendix II

or the Nunc Dimittis, *shall be sung, during which the ministers shall go out, carrying with them the Bible, the gifts of the people, the vessels used for the Communion, and any of the Elements used for the Sacrament which may remain unconsumed. These may be reverently consumed in the vestry.*

APPENDIX II

BIBLIOGRAPHY

The bibliography which follows consists for the most part simply of official sources and documents. Controversial or apologetic pamphlets concerned with the South Indian Church (of which there exists a considerable number) have not been included.

Report of the Lambeth Conference, 1930 (S.P.C.K., 2*s.* 6*d.* net).

Proposed Scheme of Church Union in South India, 7th Edition, reprinted with additional matter on pp. 22 and 90–96 (Christian Literature Society for India, Madras, 1947).

Chronicle of the Convocation of Canterbury, May 1943 (S.P.C.K., London, W.C. 2). Contains an address by the late Archbishop William Temple on *Christian Unity and Church Reunion.*

Chronicle of the Convocation of Canterbury, January 1944 (S.P.C.K., London, W.C. 2). Contains on pp. 114 *sqq.* the formal reply sent, with a covering letter, by the late Archbishop William Temple to questions formally put to him as Metropolitan of the Province of Canterbury by the then Metropolitan of India (Dr. Hubback).

Chronicle of the Convocation of Canterbury, May 1945 (S.P.C.K., London, W.C. 2). Contains the Statement on the Scheme for *Church Union in South India* made in the Full Synod of the Convocation on 15th May, 1945, by the Archbishop of Canterbury (Dr. Fisher).

The Church of South India

The South India Church Scheme. Being the Report of a Committee of Theologians appointed by the Archbishop of Canterbury (Press and Publications Board of the Church Assembly, Church House, Westminster, S.W. 1, 1946. Pp. 46. 2s.).

Church Union in South India : Its Progress and Consummation. By A. J. Arangaden (Basel Mission Press, Bangalore. 1947. Pp. 254).

The South India Church : An Open Letter from the Archbishop of Canterbury to Bishop Stephen Neill. (Press and Publications Board of the Church Assembly, Church House, Westminster, S.W. 1. 1947. 6d.)

The Reunion of the Church. By J. E. Lesslie Newbigin, Bishop in Madura and Ramnad (S.C.M. Press. 1948. Pp. 192. 10s. 6d. net).

Lambeth Conference 1948 (S.P.C.K. 5s. net).

The Church of South India : Being the United Report of the Joint Committees of the Convocations of Canterbury and York (Church Information Board, 1950. Pp. 71. 2s. 6d.).

Documents dealing with the relations between the Church of South India and the Anglican Communion (printed at Madras, India, by Fenn Thompson and Co. 8d.).

Order of Service for the Inauguration of the Church of South India, with the Form of Consecrating the First New Bishops and the Order of Service for the Ordination of Presbyters (United Society for Christian Literature, Lutterworth Press, London and Redhill. 1s. net).

Church of South India : Order of Service for the Reception of Baptised Persons into the Full Membership of the Church commonly called Confirmation (Fenn Thompson and Co., Madras).

Liturgy of the Church of South India (Oxford University Press, 1950)

Problems of Reunion. By A. E. J. Rawlinson, Bishop of Derby (Eyre and Spottiswoode, 1950. Pp. 179. 9s. net).

2